Introduction

According to the ONS (office of national statistics) there are over 30 million people in employment in the UK. Available data and statistics suggest that approximately 3.3 million people in the UK express dissatisfaction with their current jobs and wish to resign or change their employment situation.

In other words, 10%+ of the workforce are dissatisfied in their current job, role or position and may wish to resign, transform their career, or reclaim their life. What about you?

This book is for you or anyone feeling stuck, unfulfilled, or uncertain in their current job situation. Whether you're a recent graduate, a mid-career professional, or someone looking to make a drastic career change, this book is for you.

By reading, relating, assimilating, and applying the principles shared within these pages, you'll gain the courage, clarity, and confidence needed to break free from the shackles of fear, struggle, and limitation.

It's time to resign with confidence and reclaim your power to create the future you want.

Is this you?

- Are you ready to break free from the shackles of fear, uncertainty, and limitation?

- Do you crave a career that brings you joy, purpose, and meaning?

- Do you want to get on point, on form and on fire and reclaim your life?

If so, the following pages could inspire you to leave your job, transform your career and reclaim your life with the help, guidance and offer of support contained within. However, just reading this book will <u>not</u> help you create the lifestyle and joy you want, but I do have a solution.

 **When you see this symbol throughout the book. Pause & reflect. Make notes, Answer the Question or Complete the exercise. This will assist you to make the right decision for you (and your family).**

When it comes to your life, career, or business, it's now time to identify who is holding you back and preventing the confidence, progress, and future that you want. Let's make it happen.

Onwards and upwards

Fraser J. Hay

February 2024

Table of Contents

It's not always about the money.

There can be many reasons for wanting to resign from your current job, role or position, and whilst I want to cover many of the reasons later in the book (including the money), however, in this chapter I want to talk about the people you work with or work for that irritate you, get you down or really wind you up that can often act as the catalyst in you deciding to resign.

For me over the years in various roles, I've encountered a variety of personalities, each with its own unique impact on my personal and professional life. From the supportive mentor to the toxic energy vampire, recognizing and understanding these characters is crucial to navigating the workplace effectively.

Identifying these individuals and being aware of their influence can empower you to make informed decisions about your career path. The 12 different characters at work that can cause you to resign encompass a range of behaviours, from inspiring and uplifting to draining and demoralizing.

By recognizing their traits and understanding their potential impact on your mental, physical, and emotional well-being, you can take proactive steps to mitigate negative influences and create a more fulfilling work environment.

Whether it's the micromanager stifling your autonomy or the toxic coworker spreading negativity, being aware of these characters can serve as a catalyst for positive change in your career journey. By identifying the characters shaping your workplace experience, you can reclaim your sense of agency and confidently pursue a path aligned with your goals and values.

Let me introduce you to the cast of characters you already know, distrust, or want to avoid at work that may just be one of the major contributory factors in you wanting to resign, change job, transform your career, or reclaim your life:

The Micro manager

A Micro manager is the supervisor who hovers over your shoulder, scrutinizing every move and decision you make. Imagine Max, the engineering team lead, who insists on approving even the smallest details of your projects, stifling creativity, and autonomy. Their constant need for control creates a suffocating work environment, leaving you feeling frustrated and undervalued.

Despite your efforts to excel, you're met with micromanagement at every turn, leading to a loss of confidence and motivation. This overbearing management style can become the catalyst for resigning, as you yearn for the freedom to highlight your skills and make decisions independently.

Recognising the impact of micromanagers and seeking a healthier work environment where trust and empowerment thrive is essential for reclaiming your professional autonomy and confidence.

Do you really want to keep collaborating with people like Max?

Toxic Colleague

This is someone in the workplace whose negative behavior and attitude poison the environment, affecting the mental and emotional well-being of those around them. Take Alex, a software engineer, who constantly belittles his coworkers' ideas and spreads rumours about them to gain favor with management.

His toxic behaviour creates an atmosphere of distrust and hostility, making it difficult for his team to collaborate effectively. Over time, dealing with a toxic colleague like Alex can lead to increased stress, decreased job satisfaction, and resignation.

Their presence not only undermines team morale but also hinders productivity and innovation. Recognizing and addressing toxic behavior in the workplace is essential for fostering a positive and supportive work environment conducive to personal and professional growth.

Who does Alex remind you of?

Office Gossip

Ah, that colleague who thrives on spreading rumours, stirring up drama, and sharing confidential information about others in the workplace. Meet Rosemary, a clerical assistant, who spends her lunch breaks whispering in the break room about her coworkers' personal lives and work performance. She often twists facts to suit her own narrative, creating tension and mistrust among team members.

Rosemary's behaviour not only damages professional relationships but also undermines morale and productivity.

The constant fear of being the next target of her gossip can lead to anxiety and stress among colleagues, driving some to resign in search of a more positive and supportive work environment. Recognising and addressing the harmful effects of office gossip is crucial for maintaining a healthy and respectful workplace culture.

Do you really want to keep collaborating with people like Rosemary?

Credit Thief

James is that colleague who consistently takes credit for others' work, leaving the real contributors feeling undervalued and demotivated. Working in a large IT department, he often presents ideas and solutions in team meetings that were generated by his colleagues during brainstorming sessions.

By stealing the limelight and failing to acknowledge the efforts of his team members, James undermines trust and collaboration within the team. This behaviour not only damages morale but also stifles innovation and creativity.

Over time, the frustration of being consistently overlooked and unrecognised can lead talented employees like Phillip to resign in search of a workplace where their contributions are deeply appreciated. Recognising and addressing credit theft is essential for fostering a culture of fairness, respect, and teamwork in the workplace.

Ever met someone like James? Well, it's time to say "Bye. Bye James."

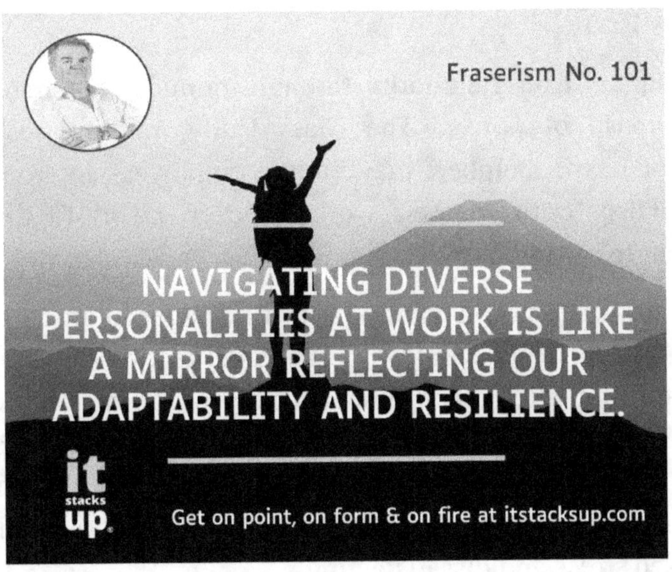

Subtle Saboteur

Oh yes, this is the passive-aggressive co-worker who undermines productivity and morale through indirect and often covert means. This individual may appear friendly and cooperative on the surface but engages in behaviours aimed at sabotaging others' efforts or causing conflict.

For example, they might subtly criticise colleagues' ideas in meetings, withhold important information, or conveniently "forget" to follow up on tasks assigned to them. The Subtle Saboteur's actions can create a toxic work environment, erode trust among team members, and drive talented employees to resign in frustration.

Their passive-aggressive behavior stems from underlying insecurities, jealousy, or a desire for control. Identifying and addressing these behaviors early on is crucial to maintaining a positive work culture and preventing valuable employees from seeking opportunities elsewhere.

There's more to life than having to deal with this kind of BS, don't you think?

The Class Bully

This individual exerts authority through intimidation, manipulation, and the abuse of power. The Class Bully, (an upline manager, superior or board member) may belittle employees in front of their peers, unfairly criticize their work, or even resort to threats and harassment to assert control.

For instance, imagine Stewart, a project manager in an oil company, whose boss, Cheryl, employs aggressive tactics such as public humiliation and micromanagement. Cheryl's constant criticism and undermining behaviour create a toxic work environment that affects Stewart's confidence and morale. Despite Stewart's dedication and hard work, he constantly feels demoralized and undervalued, leading to increased stress and dissatisfaction.

The toxic relationship with his boss becomes the driving force behind Stewart's decision to resign, as he realises that his mental well-being and career growth are being compromised. Recognizing the signs of a bully boss and taking proactive steps to address the situation is crucial for individuals like Stewart to regain control of their careers and pursue opportunities where they can thrive professionally and personally.

There's always one, isn't there?

The Chronic Complainer

I'm sure you've met or worked with someone like this. It embodies an individual who habitually voices grievances and negativity about work-related matters. Picture Helen, a marketing coordinator in a multinational corporation, whose colleague, David, constantly complains about the workload, company policies, and management decisions.

David's perpetual negativity creates a toxic atmosphere, draining morale and productivity. Despite Helen's attempts to maintain a positive outlook, the constant barrage of complaints takes a toll on her mental well-being and job satisfaction. Over time, Helen finds herself feeling increasingly demotivated and disengaged, eventually leading her to contemplate resigning from her position.

Dealing with chronic complainers like David requires resilience and assertiveness to maintain focus and positivity amidst the negativity. Recognising the impact of chronic complaining on personal well-being and career satisfaction is essential for individuals like Helen to reclaim their professional happiness and thrive in a supportive work environment.

What's holding you back from living the life and lifestyle you want?

The Unreliable

This type of colleague, co-worker or boss can be a significant source of frustration and stress. This individual has a penchant for inconsistency, often failing to deliver on commitments or meet deadlines.

Their unpredictability creates a ripple effect, impacting team morale and productivity. For instance, imagine Tony, a marketing assistant at a bustling advertising agency, relying on their colleague, Jo, a graphic designer, to complete crucial design tasks for an upcoming campaign.

However, Jo frequently misses deadlines, leaving Tony scrambling to cover her workload and jeopardizing project timelines. The constant uncertainty and unmet expectations can lead to feelings of frustration, anxiety, and disillusionment with the job.

As a result, individuals like Tony may consider resigning to escape the strain of collaborating with an unreliable co-worker and seek a more stable and supportive work environment where their efforts are valued and respected.

Do you deliver on time, within budget and without quibble? (So, what's next for you.)

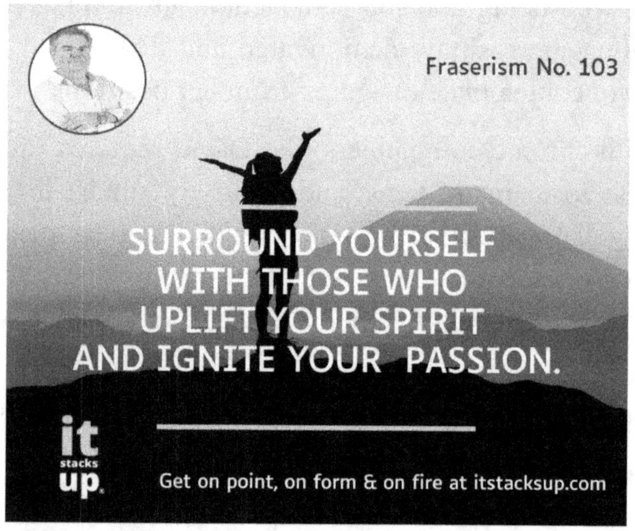

Overbearing mentor

This is someone in a senior position who exerts excessive control or dominance over their mentee, stifling their growth and autonomy. This type of mentor may micromanage tasks, dismiss the mentee's ideas, or impose their own agenda without considering the mentee's goals and aspirations.

For example, in a social media agency, a seasoned strategist might constantly override their junior colleague's decisions, hindering their ability to learn and contribute creatively. Emotionally, mentees may feel frustrated, demotivated, and undervalued, leading to a sense of disillusionment and disengagement from their role.

An overbearing mentor can become a driving force behind someone's decision to resign as it undermines their confidence, stifles their professional development, and erodes their job satisfaction.

Cue that old Clash song from the 1980s… "Should I stay or should I go."

The discriminatory colleague

Ever worked with someone who demonstrates prejudice or bias towards others based on factors such as race, gender, age, or religion. This behaviour creates a toxic work environment that can have detrimental effects on employees' well-being and job satisfaction.

Imagine a scenario where a colleague consistently undermines the contributions of a female coworker during meetings because of her gender. (Believe me, it can happen)

This discriminatory behavior not only erodes the affected employee's confidence and morale but also creates feelings of frustration, anger, and alienation.

 Over time, dealing with such discrimination can lead employees to feel demoralized and undervalued, prompting them to consider resigning in search of a more inclusive and respectful workplace. This decision may stem from a desire to escape the negative environment and find a professional setting where they are treated with fairness and respect.

Energy Vampire"

Know someone like that in your workplace? The person who constantly drains the positive energy and enthusiasm of those around them. They tend to be pessimistic, critical, and always seem to have a problem for every solution.

What if you had a colleague named Troy who works as a project manager in an IT Consultancy? Despite being part of a collaborative team environment, Troy consistently shoots down ideas, complains about workload, and spreads negativity during meetings. His cynical attitude and constant complaining create a toxic atmosphere that saps the motivation and morale of his coworkers.

Over time, dealing with Troy's negative energy can lead to increased stress, frustration, and even burnout for those collaborating closely with him. Eventually, the continuous exposure to such negativity can become unbearable, prompting employees to consider resigning in search of a more positive and supportive work environment where their contributions are appreciated and valued.

Do you know anyone like "No joy Troy"?

For me, a cup of water can either be half full or half empty, but you can always refill it.

The Career Climber.

You are bound to have met someone like this. It's someone in the workplace who is solely focused on advancing their own career, often at the expense of others. They are ambitious, competitive, and willing to do whatever it takes to get ahead, even if it means stepping on their colleagues or disregarding ethical boundaries.

For instance, consider Elaine, a sales executive in a SAAS technology company. She constantly undermines her coworkers by taking credit for their ideas, sabotaging their projects, and forming alliances with higher-ups to secure promotions.

Elaine's relentless pursuit of success creates a cutthroat environment where trust is nonexistent, and teamwork is rare. Collaborating with her can be emotionally draining and demoralising, as her self-serving behavior erodes morale and stifles collaboration.

Eventually, the toxic atmosphere created by career climbers like Elaine can push employees to resign in search of a workplace culture that values integrity, cooperation, and mutual respect.

There's no need to invest in a Kevlar stab-proof vest. Focus on your own career path.

Reflect on your current work environment and the people you interact with regularly. Identify individuals who may be affecting your physical, mental, and spiritual well-being.

Make a list of their names, along with specific behaviours or interactions that impact you negatively. Once you've identified these factors, brainstorm proactive steps you can take to address these challenges, whether it's setting boundaries, seeking support from colleagues or supervisors, or exploring opportunities for personal growth and development outside of work.

By recognising and addressing these influences, you can take control of your well-being and focus on transforming your career and reclaiming your life.

Assess Your Current Situation

As you embark on the journey of reshaping your career and reclaiming your life, it's essential to begin by assessing your current situation. In this chapter, we'll discuss this initial step and how it serves as the foundation upon which you'll build your path to success.

Now, why is it crucial to weigh up the pros and cons of your current job? Well, imagine you're a skilled architect designing a new building. Before you lay the foundation, you meticulously analyze the site's strengths and weaknesses, ensuring a solid structure. Similarly, by evaluating the positives and negatives of your job, you can make informed decisions about your career path, avoiding pitfalls and maximizing opportunities for growth.

Feeling on point, on form, and on fire are paramount to your personal well-being and professional success. Let's break down what each of these entails:

Feeling "on point" means being in alignment with your passions, values, and skills. It's about operating within your zone of genius, where your talents shine brightest. Being "on form" signifies performing at your peak level of productivity and efficiency. It's about harnessing your capabilities to deliver exceptional results consistently. Finally, being "on fire" encapsulates a state of enthusiasm, motivation, and passion for your work. It's that spark within you that ignites excitement and propels you toward your goals with unwavering determination.

Why does all this matter for your personal well-being? Well, your career (whether you work for an employer or in your own business) isn't just a series of tasks or responsibilities—it's an integral part of your identity and fulfillment. Just as a plant requires nourishment and sunlight to thrive, you need a conducive environment and a sense of purpose to flourish. Assessing your current situation empowers you to cultivate a career path that aligns with your values, passions, and aspirations, leading to greater fulfillment and satisfaction in both your personal and professional life.

For me, assessing your current situation is the first step toward crafting a career that brings you joy, fulfillment, and success. By weighing up the pros and cons, understanding what it means to feel on point, on form, and on fire, and prioritising your personal well-being, you lay the groundwork for a transformative journey toward resigning with confidence, transform your career and reclaiming your life.

Ready for the best decision you've ever made?

Evaluating your job satisfaction and dissatisfaction.

When it comes to doing this, it's vital to think about whether you are also enjoying and benefiting from meaningful work too. It's also essential to approach it with a clear and structured mindset. Think of it as conducting a thorough examination of your professional landscape to identify areas of fulfillment and areas that may need improvement.

Let's take Cath, for example. She works as a marketing coordinator at a fast-paced tech startup. At first, she was thrilled by the dynamic environment and the opportunity to work with innovative technology. However, over time, Cath began to feel increasingly dissatisfied. She found herself constantly overwhelmed by tight deadlines and high-pressure projects, leading to burnout and a lack of enthusiasm for her work. Despite the rewards of the job, such as flexible hours and catered lunches, Cath realised that these factors couldn't compensate for the lack of alignment between her values and the company's culture.

Now consider Mark, a graphic designer at a nonprofit organisation dedicated to environmental conservation. Mark is passionate about using his creative skills to make a positive impact on the world. Every day, he feels a sense of fulfillment knowing that his work contributes to a cause he deeply cares about. Although the salary may not be as high as in the corporate world, Mark finds meaning in his job that goes beyond financial compensation. He feels valued and appreciated by his colleagues and derives a sense of purpose from the meaningful projects he works on.

So, let's break down the process of evaluating job satisfaction, dissatisfaction, and meaningful work. It involves reflecting on various aspects of your job, such as the tasks you perform, the work environment, relationships with colleagues and supervisors, opportunities for growth and development, and alignment with personal values and interests.

When assessing job satisfaction, it's essential to consider what aspects of your job bring you joy, fulfillment, and a sense of accomplishment. These could include tasks that challenge you, opportunities for creativity and innovation, supportive relationships with coworkers, recognition for your contributions, and a healthy work-life balance.

On the other hand, when evaluating job dissatisfaction, it's crucial to identify any factors that detract from your overall satisfaction and well-being. These could range from job-related stress and burnout to conflicts with coworkers or supervisors, lack of opportunities for advancement, feeling undervalued or unappreciated, or a mismatch between your values and the company culture.

Lastly, assessing meaningful work involves determining whether your job aligns with your values, passions, and long-term goals. It's about finding a sense of purpose and fulfillment in what you do, knowing that your work has a positive impact on others or contributes to something greater than yourself. This could involve working for a cause you believe in, using your skills to help others, or pursuing a career path that aligns with your personal values and interests.

Evaluating your job satisfaction, dissatisfaction, and meaningful work is something I offer in FREE strategy call to help you start reclaiming your life. By taking the time to reflect on these aspects of your job, you can gain clarity on what truly matters to you and make informed decisions about your career path moving forward.

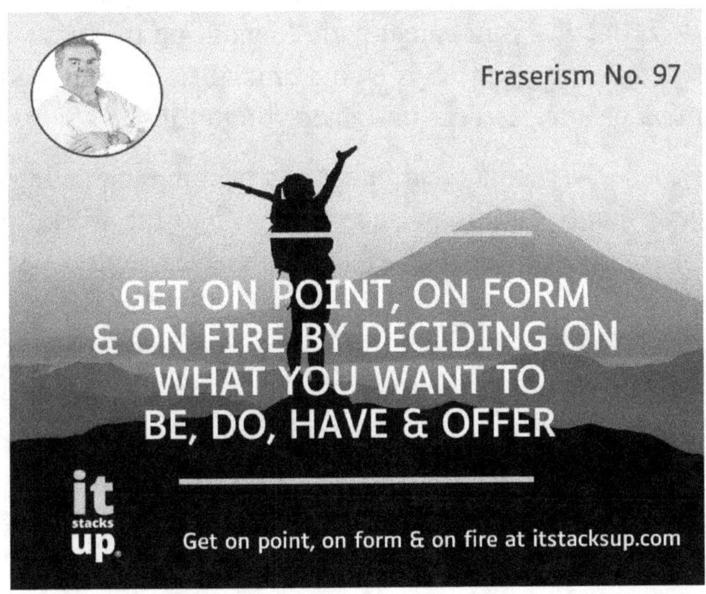

Take a moment to assess your current job by creating a "Likes, Dislikes, and Hates" list. Divide a piece of paper into three columns and jot down aspects of your job that you like, dislike, and hate.

Reflect on whether you feel valued, appreciated, and well-compensated for your contributions. Consider whether your work aligns with your values and provides a sense of fulfillment.

Additionally, evaluate whether you're enjoying meaningful work that resonates with your interests and aspirations. This exercise will help you gain clarity on your current job satisfaction levels and empower you to take proactive steps towards creating a career that brings you joy and fulfillment.

Identifying the Reasons for Wanting to Leave Your Job:

So, you're at a point where you're considering waving goodbye to your current job, yes? Well, first off, kudos to you for taking a moment to reflect on your career path. Identifying the reasons behind your desire to leave your job is also a crucial step in paving the way for your next chapter. Let me introduce you to Lily and Sam.

Meet Lily, a social media coordinator at a bustling marketing agency. Lily initially jumped at the chance to dive into the world of digital marketing, eager to flex her creative muscles and connect with audiences online. However, as time passed, Lily found herself feeling increasingly drained and unfulfilled by her role. The constant pressure to churn out content at breakneck speed and maintain a flawless online presence took a toll on her mental health. Despite her best efforts to stay afloat, Lily realized that the job was no longer serving her well-being.

Now, let me introduce you to Sam, a financial analyst at a prestigious investment firm. Sam was drawn to the allure of Wall Street and the promise of lucrative opportunities in the world of finance. However, as he delved deeper into his role, Sam began to feel like a cog in the corporate machine, crunching numbers day in and day out without a sense of purpose or passion. The long hours and high-stakes pressure left him feeling burnt out and disconnected from his true interests and values. Sam knew that he needed to find a career path that aligned with his passions and allowed him to make a meaningful impact.

So, what are some common reasons why people may want to leave their jobs?

Let's explore:

Lack of Alignment with Personal Values. Feeling like your job doesn't align with your core values can be a major red flag. Whether it's ethical concerns, a clash with company culture, or simply feeling out of sync with your organization's mission, recognizing this misalignment is crucial in determining whether it's time to move on.

Limited Opportunities for Growth and Development. Feeling like you're stuck in a rut with no room to grow or advance can be incredibly frustrating. If your current job lacks opportunities for learning, skill development, or career progression, it may be holding you back from reaching your full potential.

Work-Life Imbalance. Struggling to maintain a healthy balance between work and personal life can take a toll on your overall well-being.

If your job demands long hours, constant availability, or frequent travel, leaving you with little time for rest, relaxation, or meaningful connections outside of work, it may be a sign that your priorities are out of whack.

Feeling Unfulfilled or Uninspired. Life's too short to spend your days feeling bored, uninspired, or unfulfilled by your work. If you find yourself dreading going to work each day or feeling like you're just going through the motions without any sense of passion or purpose, it may be a sign that it's time to seek out new opportunities that light a fire in your soul.

Toxic Work Environment. Dealing with a toxic work environment characterized by conflict, negativity, or hostility can have a significant impact on your mental and emotional well-being. If you find yourself feeling stressed, anxious, or drained by your interactions with coworkers or supervisors, it may be necessary to remove yourself from the situation for the sake of your health and happiness.

Identifying the reasons for wanting to leave your job is an essential step in reclaiming your career and your life. By taking the time to reflect on your motivations and assess your current situation, you can gain clarity on what you need to thrive and move forward with confidence in your decision.

Which of the following reasons for leaving, resonate with you:

• Limited opportunities for career advancement	• inadequate pay, compensation, or benefits
• Unhealthy work-life balance	• Boredom and lack of challenge in the role
• Cultural misalignment with the organization	• Commuting or location issues affecting quality of life.
• Toxic work environment or interpersonal conflicts	• Personal or family reasons require flexibility.
• Lack of recognition or appreciation for contributions	• Feeling undervalued or unfulfilled in the role
• High levels of stress and burnout	• Desire for a career change or pursuit of new opportunities
• Inadequate compensation or benefits	

Write down your reasons for wanting to leave your current job. Be specific and honest about what motivates your desire for change. Whether it's a lack of growth opportunities, toxic work culture, or a misalignment with your values, identify the key factors driving your decision.

Consider examples such as feeling undervalued despite your contributions, experiencing burnout from excessive workload, or seeking greater work-life balance. By articulating your reasons clearly, you'll gain clarity on your career goals and be better equipped to pursue opportunities that align with your values and aspirations.

Understanding the Impact of Your Job on Various Aspects of Your Life:

It's vital that you understand that we humans are emotional beings, and whilst feelings create circumstances. Circumstances can and do create emotions which can manifest in various forms in our work, relationships, and health.

Your job isn't just about the work you do from 9 to 5. It can influence everything from your health and relationships to your overall happiness and well-being. So, let's take a closer look at how your job might be affecting various aspects of your life, shall we?

Meet Emily, a graphic designer at a small design agency. Emily loves her job and feels incredibly passionate about the projects she works on. However, lately, she's been feeling stressed and overwhelmed by the constant pressure to meet tight deadlines. This stress has started to spill over into other areas of her life, affecting her sleep, mood, and overall sense of well-being. Emily realises that she needs to find a way to manage her workload more effectively to prevent it from taking a toll on her health and happiness.

The impact of our working environment affects each of us in different ways.

Let me introduce you to Alex, for example, a sales executive at a large corporate firm. Alex is dedicated to his career and has worked hard to climb the corporate ladder. However, he's starting to feel like he's sacrificing too much of his personal life for his job. Long hours and frequent business trips have taken a toll on his relationships with his family and friends. Alex recognizes that he needs to find a better balance between his work commitments and his personal life to maintain healthy connections with the people who matter most to him.

So, what are some of the ways your job can impact different aspects of your life?

Let's break it down:

Physical Health. Your job can have a significant impact on your physical health. Long hours spent sitting at a desk or engaging in repetitive tasks can lead to issues like back pain, eye strain, and fatigue. Additionally, high levels of stress and pressure can weaken your immune system and increase your risk of developing chronic health conditions like heart disease and diabetes.

Mental Health. Your job can also affect your mental health. Dealing with high levels of stress, pressure, and uncertainty can lead to feelings of anxiety, depression, and burnout. Additionally, toxic work environments characterized by bullying, harassment, or micromanagement can take a toll on your mental well-being and overall quality of life.

Relationships. Your job can impact your relationships with others. Long hours, unpredictable schedules, and frequent travel can make it challenging to spend quality time with your family and friends. Additionally, work-related stress and conflicts can strain your relationships and lead to communication breakdowns and resentment.

Financial Well-Being. Your job plays a significant role in your financial well-being. A stable job with a competitive salary and benefits can provide you with financial security and peace of mind. However, job instability, inadequate compensation, or unexpected expenses can create financial stress and uncertainty.

Work-Life Balance. Achieving a healthy work-life balance is essential for your overall well-being. Balancing the demands of work with personal commitment and self-care allows you to recharge and maintain a sense of fulfillment outside of the office. However, excessive work demands, or a lack of boundaries can lead to burnout, fatigue, and decreased satisfaction with both work and personal life.

Understanding the impact of your job on various aspects of your life is essential for making informed decisions about your career path. By recognising how your job influences your physical health, mental well-being, relationships, financial stability, and work-life balance, you can assess whether your current role aligns with your overall goals and priorities. Remember, your job should enhance your life, not detract from it. So, take the time to reflect on how your job affects different areas of your well-being and make choices that prioritize your happiness and fulfillment.

Take a moment to assess the impact your current job, role, or position is having on your mental, physical, and financial well-being. Reflect on how your job affects your stress levels, energy levels, and overall happiness.

Consider examples such as feeling constantly stressed or anxious, experiencing physical symptoms like headaches or fatigue, or struggling with financial stability due to low pay or excessive expenses.

By acknowledging the ways in which your job may be impacting your well-being, you'll be empowered to take proactive steps to prioritize self-care and seek out opportunities that promote a healthier work-life balance.

Seek Clarity, Vision & Purpose

Imagine having a clear picture of what you want to be, what you want to do, and what you want to have in both your personal and professional life. It's important because often we get embattled with our problems, pains, frustrations, and the daily challenges presented in the workplace. We need to remind ourselves where we are, and what it is we want and why.

For me, the meaning of life is to discover your gift, and the purpose of life is to share it. More importantly, if you want to get on point, on form and fire then you need to complete this wee exercise.

 **Write down your answer to these 3 questions. What are you good at? What do you enjoy doing? If you had no chance of failure, what would you do next with your life? Take as long as you need.**

At this point, I want to say something a little controversial…

You are **not** a human being; you are a human becoming.

The question is what do you want to become? There's 3 parts to help fire up your engine of desire and help to keep you focused on wanting to resign from your current job. role or position.

Later, we'll look at 3 parts to this, but for just now what "job title" would you like to have, and OK, dare I say it, how much salary do you want and why.

Whatever it is, having a clear vision of the role or job title you want to be can guide your actions and decisions in both your personal and professional life.

Next up, let's talk about what you want to do. This is where we get into the nitty-gritty of your career goals and aspirations. Do you dream of starting your own business, climbing the corporate ladder, or making a career change into a field you're passionate about?

More importantly, that is the value of the wisdom, skills, talent, and contacts you have collected over the years that you can share with potential employers (or potentially clients.)

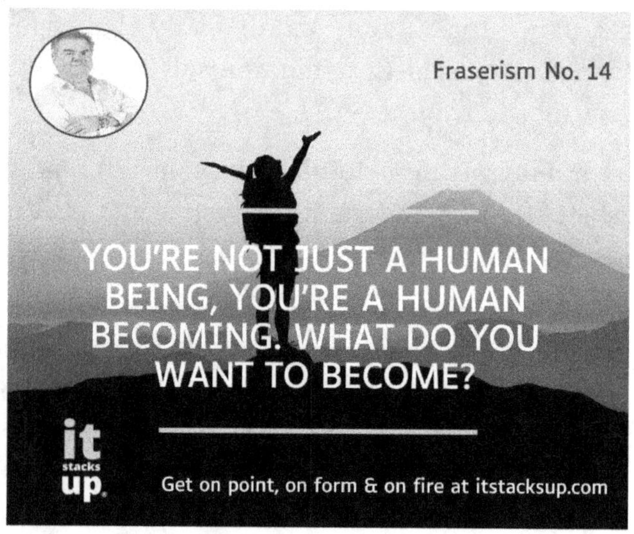

Another wee exercise for you.

Take a moment to reflect on the number of years that have passed since you landed your first full-time job until today. Write down this number.

Next, calculate your average annual salary over that period by adding up the total income earned and dividing it by the number of years worked. Write down this figure.

Finally, multiply the number of years worked by your average annual salary to determine the total value of your intellectual capital.

This exercise highlights the cumulative value of your skills, knowledge, and experience gained over your career journey, empowering you to recognise the significance of your intellectual capital in shaping your professional worth and future opportunities.

WOW, that's an asset you probably didn't even realise you owned. Unlike stocks, shares, or property, that valuable asset is your intellectual capital that you can offer to anyone who is prepared to pay you for the value you offer, and for many it can be 10% of that figure per annum (or higher). It might be lower; it all depends on how serious you want to get.

Whatever your career aspirations may be, having a clear vision of what you want to achieve professionally can help you stay focused, motivated, and on track to reaching your goals.

Now, let's talk about what you want to have. This could be anything from financial stability and a comfortable lifestyle to meaningful relationships and a sense of fulfillment. What do you want your life to look like? What do you want to have achieved by the time you retire? By clarifying what you want to have in your life, you can set meaningful goals and take steps to make your dreams a reality.

But here's the thing: it's not just about knowing what you want. It's also about having the desire, belief, and expectation that you can achieve it. When you have a burning desire for your goals, a strong belief in yourself and your abilities, and an unwavering expectation of success, you become unstoppable. You're on point, on form, and on fire with your career objectives, ready to tackle any challenge that comes your way.

Remember, in order to receive the salary, benefits of compensation you want, you need to think very carefully about the value you offer and the tasks and services you can complete on time, within budget and without quibble.

So, are you ready to gain clarity, vision, and purpose in your life and career? Are you ready to unleash your full potential and create the life and career of your dreams?

If so, get ready to ignite your passion, unleash your potential, and start a next chapter in your life…

Defining Your Long-Term Career Goals and Aspirations

Having a clear vision of where you want to be, do, and have is one thing, but It's about setting your sights on your future path and taking intentional steps to turn your dreams into reality. So, let's explore how you can define your long-term career goals and aspirations, shall we?

Meet Mia, a recent graduate with a degree in environmental science. Mia has always been passionate about protecting the planet and making a positive impact on the environment. Her long-term career goal is to become a leading environmental scientist, conducting groundbreaking research and advocating for sustainable practices in the industry. To achieve her aspirations, Mia plans to pursue a master's degree in environmental science, gain direct experience through internships and research projects, and build a strong network of mentors and peers in the field.

Know anyone like Mia? What about Neil?

Let me introduce you to Alex, a software developer with an IT consultancy. Alex loves coding and building innovative solutions that solve real-world problems. His long-term career goal is to start his own software development company, where he can create innovative technology and lead a team of talented engineers. To achieve his goals and objectives, Alex plans to gain valuable experience in the tech industry, hone his leadership skills, and learn about entrepreneurship through courses and mentorship programs.

So, how can you define your long-term career goals and aspirations?

Reflect on Your Passions and Values. Take some time to reflect on what truly matters to you and what you're passionate about. Think about the activities, subjects, or causes that energize and inspire you.

By aligning your career goals with your passions and values, you can find greater fulfillment and purpose in your work.

Set SMART Goals Yes, that old chestnut. When defining your long-term career goals, it's important to make them SMART: Specific, Measurable, Achievable, Relevant, and Time-bound. Instead of saying, "I want to be successful," be specific about what success looks like to you and how you'll measure it.

Break It Down into Milestones. Achieving your long-term career goals can feel overwhelming if you try to tackle them all at once. Break them down into smaller, manageable milestones or objectives that you can work toward incrementally. Celebrate your progress along the way and adjust your course as needed.

Seek Inspiration and Guidance. Look to successful individuals in your industry or field for inspiration and guidance. Read biographies, listen to podcasts, and attend networking events to learn from their experiences and insights. Seek out mentors who can provide valuable advice and support as you pursue your goals.

Stay Flexible and Adapt. Life is full of twists and turns, and your career path may not always follow a straight line. Stay flexible and open-minded and be willing to adapt to changing circumstances or new opportunities that arise along the way. Embrace the journey and trust that each experience brings you closer to your long-term career goals and aspirations.

Defining your long-term career goals and aspirations is necessary and vital in building a fulfilling and successful career.

By reflecting on your passions and values, setting SMART goals, breaking them down into milestones, seeking inspiration and guidance, staying flexible and adapting, you can create a roadmap for your professional journey.

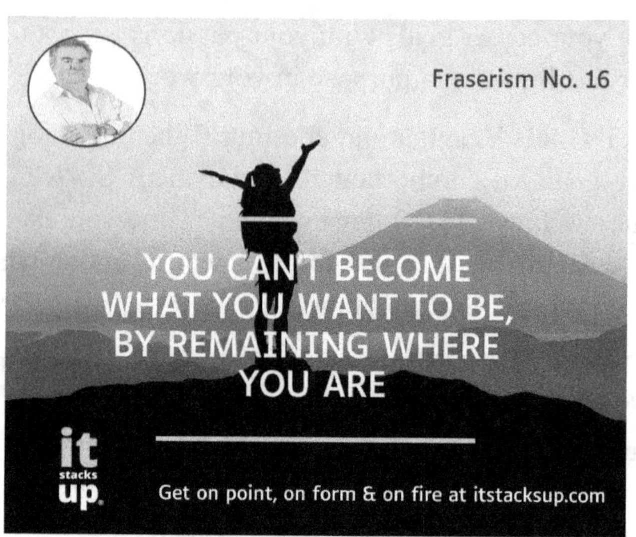

Have you planned for your retirement? Create a NET WORTH statement by writing down all your assets, and liabilities. Include things like property, shares, houses, and what you owe to whom. You might surprise yourself. How much do you need to live in retirement?

Imagine yourself in your dream job and retirement scenario, then write a detailed job description for both. For your dream job, outline the responsibilities, skills required, company culture, and impact you want to make. Be specific about the industry, position title, and potential salary.

Next, describe your ideal retirement lifestyle, including where you want to live, activities you want to enjoy, and financial security measures you want in place. By defining these long-term goals and aspirations in detail, you'll gain clarity on what you truly desire and be inspired to take actionable steps to turn these dreams into reality.

Identifying Your Skills, Strengths, and Passions

Remember earlier, I asked you 3 quick questions? Well, let's revisit the first 2…What are you good at, and enjoy doing?

Why? It's all about identifying your skills, strengths, and passions. You see, understanding what you're good at, what you enjoy doing, and what sets you apart is key to finding work that energises and fulfills you. No amount of money will make you happy if you're stuck in a job you hate. It's true. Me? I haven't worked in over 20 years, for I love what I do and enjoy helping people to identify, pursue and achieve their personal, professional, and commercial objectives.

What are your unique talents and passions?

Meet Emma, a recent college graduate with a degree in psychology. Emma has always been drawn to helping others and has a knack for listening and providing support. Through reflection and self-assessment, Emma identifies her strengths as empathy, communication, and problem-solving. She realizes that her passion lies in counseling and decides to pursue a career as a mental health counselor. With her skills and passions aligned, Emma feels confident and excited about her career path.

Marcus, a prompt engineer working at an AI startup. Marcus is passionate about coding and loves the challenge of solving complex problems. Through reflection and feedback from colleagues, Marcus identifies his skills in AI, problem-solving, and teamwork.

He realises that his strengths lie in developing and writing innovative prompt solutions and decides to pursue opportunities in AI and language models. With his skills and passions aligned, Marcus feels empowered to take his career to the next level. And you?

Self-Reflection. Take some time to reflect on your past experiences, both inside and outside of work or school. What tasks or activities do you excel at? What do you enjoy doing in your free time? By identifying patterns and themes in your experiences, you can uncover your natural talents and passions.

Feedback from Others. Seek feedback from friends, family, colleagues, and mentors about your strengths and skills. Ask them what they see as your greatest strengths and where they think you excel. Their perspectives can provide valuable insights and help you gain a better understanding of your unique abilities.

Skills Assessment Tools. Consider using skills assessment tools or personality assessments to gain a deeper understanding of your strengths and preferences. These tools can provide objective feedback and help you identify areas where you excel and areas where you may need to develop further.

Passion Projects. Engage in activities or projects that ignite your passion and enthusiasm. Whether it's volunteering, pursuing a hobby, or taking on a side project, engaging in activities that you love can help you uncover your passions and strengths.

Experimentation. Don't be afraid to try new things and step outside of your comfort zone. Experimenting with different roles, projects, or activities allows you to discover what you enjoy and what you excel at. Embrace the process of exploration and trust that each experience brings you closer to understanding yourself and your unique talents.

Identifying your skills, strengths, and passions is a critical step in building a career that brings you joy and fulfillment. By engaging in self-reflection, seeking feedback from others, using skills assessment tools, pursuing passion projects, and embracing experimentation, you can uncover your unique talents and passions and align them with your career goals.

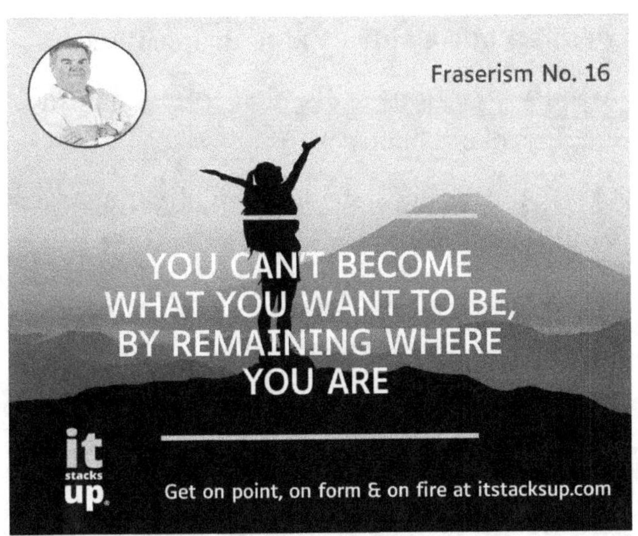

Make a comprehensive list of your technical, meta (soft), and creative skills. Draw from your past experiences, education, training, hobbies, and interests. Don't forget to calculate how much time, money, and stress you can save an employer (or client) with the valuable skills you offer.

Assess the Value of Each Skill

Evaluate how each skill contributes to achieving goals or solving problems.

Consider its impact on work performance, productivity, and project success.

Reflect on Not Utilising Your Skills.

Think about the consequences if you can't use each skill effectively.

Consider missed opportunities, decreased performance, or negative impacts.

Define Your Unique Value Proposition

Identify the top skills that offer the most value to employers or clients.

Craft a concise statement highlighting your strengths, value, and impact.

Practice communicating your value proposition confidently in various settings.

Completing this exercise provides insight into your skills, the value you offer, cost of alternate solutions, and the impact of employers not using them effectively. Use this knowledge to market yourself effectively and highlight your unique value to employers or clients. Continuously refine and update your value proposition as you progress in your career.

Exploring potential career paths aligned with your vision.

OK, so you want a change, and the reasons why. You also know what you're good at, what you enjoy doing and the value you bring to an employer. So, let's explore potential career paths and options that align with your vision and the next chapter in your career progression.

Whilst there may no longer be jobs for life, there is opportunity for life. In our mad, chaotic, and stressful world of uncertainty and the current economic climate, it is still full of endless possibilities with the right mindset and strategy. You can discover opportunities that not only align with your passions & interests but also propel you toward your long-term career goals. So, let's explore how you can uncover potential career paths and options that are in line with your vision, or some new ones, you hadn't considered?

Sheila is a recent college graduate with a degree in marketing. Sheila has always been passionate about entrepreneurship and dreams of one day starting her own marketing agency. To explore potential career paths aligned with her vision, Sheila decides to take a proactive approach. She begins by researching different industries and job roles related to marketing, such as digital marketing, content creation, and branding. Through networking events, informational interviews, and online courses, Sheila gains valuable insights into the various career paths available to him. She also explores opportunities for freelancing and side hustles to gain hands-on experience and test out different aspects of the marketing industry. Armed with this knowledge, Sheila feels confident in her ability to pursue her entrepreneurial dreams while gaining valuable experience along the way.

But what about you? What options are you considering?

Now, let's introduce you to Deborah, a mid-career professional working in the healthcare industry. Deborah has been feeling unfulfilled in her current role and is eager to explore new career paths that align with her passion for helping others. After some soul-searching and reflection, Deborah identifies her strengths in leadership, problem-solving, and patient care. She begins exploring potential career paths in healthcare administration, health education, and nonprofit management. Deborah attends industry conferences, workshops, and networking events to connect with professionals in these fields and learn more about the opportunities available. She also considers pursuing further education or certifications to enhance her skills and qualifications. Through her exploration, Deborah discovers new career paths that excite and inspire her, reigniting her passion for making a difference in the healthcare industry.

So, how can you explore potential career paths and options aligned with your vision? Let's break it down:

Self-Reflection. Take some time to reflect on your passions, interests, strengths, and values. What do you enjoy doing? What are you good at? What kind of impact do you want to make in the world?

By understanding yourself better, you can narrow down potential career paths that align with your vision.

Research and Exploration. Dive into research to learn more about different industries, job roles, and career paths that interest you. Use resources such as job boards, industry publications, and professional networking sites to gather information and explore your options. Reach out to professionals in your desired field for informational interviews and insights into their career paths.

Networking and Connections. Build relationships with professionals in your desired .industry or field through networking events, industry conferences, and online communities. Connect with mentors who can provide guidance and advice as you explore potential career paths. Leverage your network on Linkedin to uncover hidden opportunities and gain valuable insights into the industry.

Experimentation and Experience. Don't be afraid to try new things and gain hands-on experience in different areas related to your vision. Consider volunteering, internships, freelance work, or side projects to test out different career paths and gain valuable skills and experience. Use these opportunities to gain experience, grow, and refine your career goals and aspirations.

Continuous Learning and Growth. Stay curious and committed to continuous learning and development. Keep up with industry trends, developments, and emerging technologies to stay relevant and competitive in your desired field. Pursue further education, certifications, or training programs to enhance your skills and qualifications and position yourself for success in your chosen career path.

Industry Immersion Programs. Participate in industry-specific immersion programs or workshops that offer direct experience and insights into different career paths. These programs often provide opportunities to shadow professionals, work on real-world projects, and gain a deeper understanding of various industries.

Career Assessments and Personality Tests. Take advantage of career assessments and personality tests designed to help individuals identify their strengths, preferences, and ideal career paths. These assessments can provide valuable insights and guidance in exploring potential career options that align with your personality, values, and interests.

Job Shadowing and Informational Interviews. Arrange job shadowing opportunities or informational interviews with professionals working in fields or roles of interest. Shadowing allows you to observe daily activities and responsibilities firsthand, while informational interviews provide an opportunity to ask questions, and gather insights.

Skills Development Webinar Courses. Attend skills development workshops, seminars, or online courses to enhance your existing skills and acquire new ones relevant to your desired career path. By investing in continuous learning and skill development, you can expand your capabilities and increase your competitiveness in the job market.

Respect & value your own intellectual capital. You could productise and monetise your intellectual capital by licensing it to 3rd parties and organisations who value what you know, have, and offer. You could also repackage your intellectual capital and offer to license it or sell it online via your own website.

Whatever you decide, exploring potential career paths and options aligned with your vision should be done, before deciding to stay or resign. By reading the "Fraserisms" in this book and completing the activities, doing research on online recruitment and job sites, facebook groups, networking, attending career events, and continuous learning, you can uncover opportunities that align with your passions, interests, and long-term career goals.

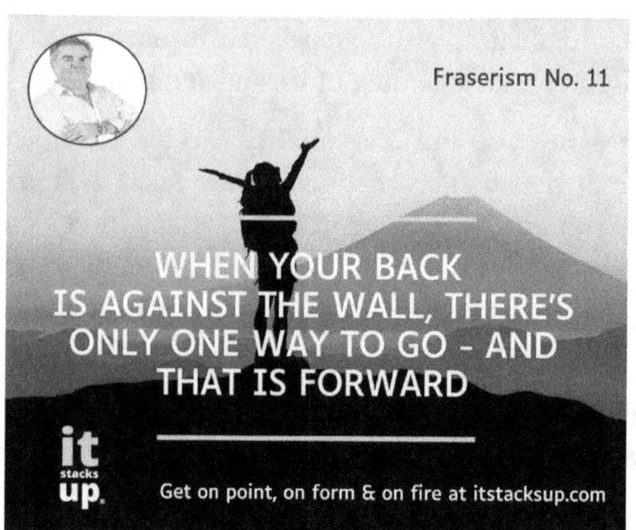

Explore potential career paths aligned with your vision by creating a career path map. Start by listing different industries or sectors that resonate with your long-term goals and aspirations.

Then, research specific roles within each industry that align with your skills, strengths, and passions. Consider factors such as job responsibilities, growth opportunities, and alignment with your values.

Finally, map out potential career trajectories for each path, identifying entry-level positions, mid-level roles, and eventual career advancements. By visualizing these potential paths, you'll gain clarity on the steps needed to achieve your career vision and feel empowered to take proactive steps towards your desired future.

Building Your Confidence

In this chapter, we'll explore the importance of confidence in navigating the process of leaving your job, transforming your career, and reclaiming your life. Confidence plays a crucial role in empowering you to take bold steps towards your goals, overcome challenges, and seize new opportunities.

Why is Confidence Important?

Confidence is like a superpower that fuels your ability to take action and achieve your aspirations. When you believe in yourself and your abilities, you're more likely to pursue your dreams with determination and resilience. Confidence enables you to step out of your comfort zone, embrace change, and push past obstacles that may arise along the way.

Embracing Change with Confidence:

Leaving your job and embarking on a new career path can be a daunting prospect, filled with uncertainty and unknowns. However, having confidence in yourself and your decisions can help alleviate fears and doubts, making the transition smoother and more manageable. With confidence as your guiding light, you'll feel empowered to embrace change as an opportunity for growth and transformation.

Unlocking Your Full Potential:

Confidence unlocks your full potential and enables you to tap into your talents, skills, and strengths. When you trust in yourself and your abilities, you're more likely to take on challenges, seize opportunities, and achieve remarkable results. Confidence propels you forward, propelling you towards your goals and dreams with unwavering determination.

Building Resilience and Overcoming Setbacks:

Confidence is not just about feeling good about yourself; it's also about building resilience in the face of adversity. Inevitably, there will be setbacks and obstacles along your career journey. However, with confidence as your foundation, you'll be better equipped to bounce back from setbacks, learn from failures, and keep moving forward with renewed determination.

Cultivating Self-Trust and Self-Empowerment:

At its core, confidence is about trusting yourself and your instincts, and believing that you have the power to shape your own destiny. When you cultivate self-trust and self-empowerment, you become the author of your own story, capable of creating the life and career you envision for yourself.

Embarking on a career change can feel like diving into the unknown. The excitement of new opportunities is often overshadowed by fears and self-doubt. However, with the right mindset and strategies, you can navigate this transition with confidence and clarity.

Fear and self-doubt are natural responses to change. They stem from uncertainty about the future and concerns about our ability to succeed in unfamiliar territory. Whether you're considering a shift to a different industry, pursuing a new role, or starting your own venture, these emotions can be powerful roadblocks if left unchecked.

Take Donald, for example, a marketing executive who dreamed of transitioning into the world of tech. Despite his passion for the industry, he found himself paralysed by fear of failure. Doubts crept in: "What if I'm not qualified enough? What if I can't keep up with the challenging environment? What if I can't find a job? I need to live and pay my bills."

These thoughts held him back from taking the leap he desperately desired.

Strategies for Overcoming Fear and Self-Doubt:

Identify Your Fears. Start by pinpointing the specific fears and doubts holding you back. Are you afraid of rejection? Worried about financial stability? By confronting these fears head-on, you can begin to disarm their power over you.

Challenge Negative Thoughts. Once you've identified your fears, challenge the validity of your negative thoughts. Ask yourself: "What evidence do I have to support these beliefs?" Often, you'll realize that your fears are based on assumptions rather than facts.

Cultivate Self-Compassion. Be kind to yourself throughout the process. Remember that it's normal to feel uncertain when venturing into uncharted territory. Practice self-compassion by offering yourself encouragement and support, just as you would to a friend facing a similar challenge.

Seek Support. Don't hesitate to lean on your network for guidance and encouragement. Reach out to mentors, peers, or career coaches who can offer valuable insights and reassurance. Surrounding yourself with positive influences can help bolster your confidence and resolve.

Take Incremental Steps. Instead of trying to tackle everything at once, break down your career change into manageable steps. Set small, achievable goals that gradually move you closer to your desired outcome. Celebrate each milestone along the way to boost your confidence and motivation.

Applying Strategies to Real-Life Situations.

Let's revisit Donald's story. After identifying his fears and challenging his negative thoughts, Donald took proactive steps to pursue his dream career in tech. He enrolled in online courses on Udemy.com to expand his skills and networked with professionals in the industry on linkedin and by attending local chamber of commerce meetings.

With the support of a coach, he gained valuable insights and encouragement, reinforcing his belief in himself. By taking incremental steps and cultivating self-compassion, Donald transformed his fears into fuel for growth. Today, he thrives working for himself as a consultant with several tech company clients, grateful for the journey that led him to transforming his career and reclaiming his life.

My point? Navigating a career change requires courage, resilience, and self-belief. By acknowledging and addressing your fears and self-doubt, you can embrace change with onfidence and clarity. Not only that, you may surprise yourself what it is you really want to to do next with your life, (and not just working for people, but collaborating with them in your own business.) Remember, you have the power to shape your future and create a career that aligns with your passions and aspirations. Trust in yourself, take bold action, and watch as new opportunities unfold on your path to finding meaningful work and success.

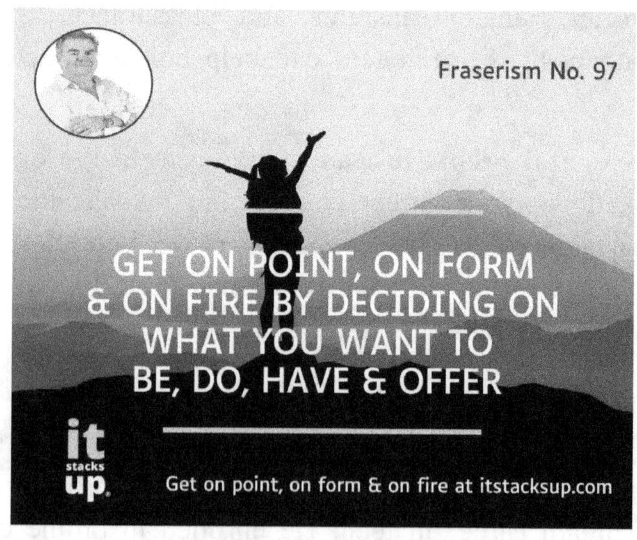

Create a vision board that represents your aspirations and dreams for your future career. Gather magazines, images, quotes, and any other visual elements that resonate with the career path you desire.

Arrange them on a board or a digital collage, focusing on the feelings of excitement, fulfillment, and success that you envision in your new role. Display your vision board in a prominent place where you'll see it daily, allowing it to serve as a powerful reminder of the possibilities that await you beyond your current job.

As you gaze upon your vision board, let it inspire you to overcome your fears, take decisive action, and step boldly into the next chapter of your career journey.

Cultivating a mindset of resilience and positivity.

Let's face it life has an uncanny knack of getting our attention when we're not paying attention, and I share examples of this in my TEDx talk and why cultivating a mindset of resilience and positivity is essential for your success whatever you choose to do in the next chapter of your life.

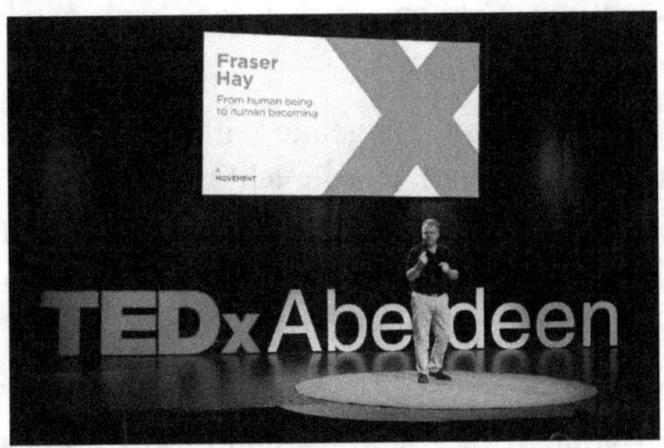

Whether you're considering leaving your current job, exploring new opportunities, or facing unexpected challenges along the way, maintaining a resilient outlook can empower you to overcome obstacles and thrive in the face of change. Let's explore how you can cultivate this mindset and harness its power to navigate your career journey with confidence and determination.

Understanding Resilience. Resilience is more than just bouncing back from setbacks; it's about adapting, learning, and growing stronger in the process. Think of it as a muscle that you can strengthen through practice and perseverance. When faced with adversity, resilient individuals maintain a positive attitude, embrace change as an opportunity for growth, and remain steadfast in pursuit of their goals.

Meet Alex:

Consider the story of Alex, a software engineer who found himself at a crossroads in his career. After years of working for a large corporation, he felt unfulfilled and yearned for a more creative and entrepreneurial path. However, the prospect of leaving his stable job and venturing into the uncertain world of freelancing filled him with doubt and anxiety.

Cultivating a Resilient Mindset. Embrace change as growth. Instead of viewing change as a threat, reframe it as an opportunity for personal and professional development. Embrace the unknown with curiosity and optimism, knowing that each new experience brings valuable lessons and insights.

Practice Self-Compassion. Be gentle with yourself during times of challenge or setback. Offer yourself the same kindness and understanding that you would to a friend facing a similar situation. Recognize that setbacks are a natural part of the journey and an opportunity for learning and growth.

Focus on Solutions, Not Problems. When confronted with obstacles, shift your focus from dwelling on the problem to seeking solutions. Approach challenges with a proactive mindset, brainstorming creative strategies and taking decisive action to overcome them.

Cultivate a Supportive Network. Surround yourself with positive influences who uplift and encourage you on your journey. Seek out mentors, peers, or coaches who can offer guidance, perspective, and support during times of uncertainty.

Practice Gratitude. Cultivate an attitude of gratitude by regularly reflecting on the things in your life that you're thankful for. Even during difficult times, focusing on the positive can help shift your perspective and bolster your resilience.

Remember Alex?

Returning to Alex's story, he recognised that cultivating a resilient mindset was key to navigating his career transition with confidence. Instead of letting fear hold him back, he embraced the opportunity for growth and self-discovery. With the support of a mentor and his network, he developed a clear plan and took incremental steps towards his goal of freelancing. Along the way, he encountered challenges and setbacks, but he approached them with resilience and determination, viewing them as opportunities for learning and growth. Today, Alex thrives as a successful freelance software developer, grateful for the resilience that carried him through the ups and downs of his career journey.

My point?

In the journey of resigning from your current job and transforming your career, cultivating a mindset of resilience and positivity is paramount. By embracing change as an opportunity for growth, practicing self-compassion, focusing on solutions, cultivating a supportive network, and practicing gratitude, you can navigate challenges with confidence and determination. Remember, resilience is not about avoiding obstacles but about facing them head-on with courage and resilience, knowing that you have the strength and resilience to overcome them and emerge stronger than ever before.

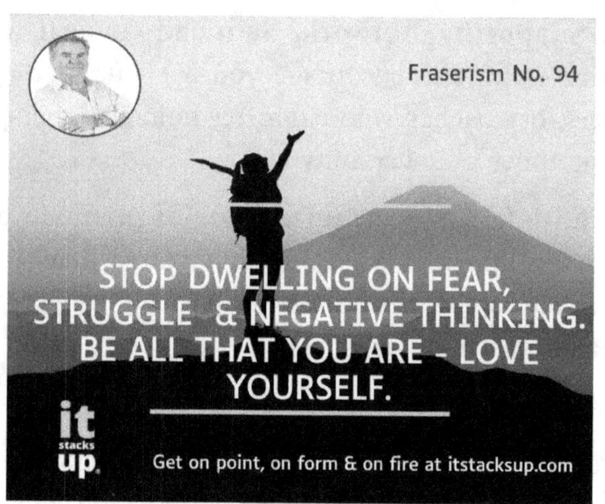

Commit to spending just five minutes each day reflecting on your resilience journey by keeping a "Daily Resilience Journal." In this journal, jot down one challenge you faced during the day and how you responded to it with resilience. Then, write down one thing you're grateful for, no matter how small.

Finally, set an intention for tomorrow, focusing on how you will approach any obstacles or setbacks with resilience and positivity. This simple practice will help reinforce the concept of resilience in your mind and empower you to take proactive steps towards building a more resilient mindset in your career journey.

I also recommend that you do watch my TEDx talk as I hope it helps to reinforce some of the points in this chapter and it might just fire up new levels of desire, belief, and expectation in yourself and what you want to do next with your career. It's here –

https://www.youtube.com/watch?v=IttJ_XNMTwU or do a google search for "Fraser Hay TEDx talk." (It's not long – about 12 mins.)

Unleashing Your Confidence: Strategies for Career Success

Let's face it. Confidence is the cornerstone of success in any career transition. Whether you're resigning from your current job, exploring new opportunities, or charting a path towards your goals, developing strategies to boost your self-confidence is essential. In this section, we'll explore practical techniques to help you cultivate unwavering confidence and unlock your full potential as you embark on your journey of transformation.

Understanding Self-Confidence. Self-confidence is not about being flawless or never experiencing self-doubt. Instead, it's about trusting in your abilities, believing in yourself, and embracing your worthiness to pursue your aspirations. When you exude confidence, you inspire trust and credibility, both crucial factors in achieving your career goals.

Meet Emily.

Know anyone like Emily? She was a graphic designer who dreamed of launching her own freelance business. Despite her talent and expertise, she struggled with self-doubt and uncertainty about her ability to succeed on her own. The fear of failure held her back from taking the leap and pursuing her entrepreneurial aspirations. More on her later, but first…

Strategies to Boost Self-Confidence:

Set SMART Goals. Start by setting Specific, Measurable, Achievable, Relevant, and Time-bound (SMART) goals that align with your career aspirations. Breaking down your objectives into actionable steps provides clarity and direction, empowering you to make progress with confidence.

Celebrate Your Achievements. Acknowledge and celebrate your accomplishments, no matter how small. Keep a journal of your successes, whether it's completing a challenging project, receiving positive feedback from a colleague, or mastering a new skill.

Reflecting on your achievements reinforces your confidence and reminds you of your capabilities.

Practice Self-Compassion. Be kind to yourself, especially during times of challenge or setback. Replace self-criticism with self-compassion, recognizing that mistakes are opportunities for growth and learning. Treat yourself with the same empathy and understanding that you would offer to a friend facing a similar situation.

Step Out of Your Comfort Zone. Challenge yourself to step out of your comfort zone and embrace new opportunities for growth. Whether it's volunteering for a leadership role, speaking up in meetings, or taking on a stretch assignment, pushing past your perceived limits builds resilience and confidence in your abilities.

Visualize Success. Harness the power of visualization by imagining yourself achieving your goals with confidence and conviction. Create a mental image of your desired outcome, envisioning every detail of your success. Visualization primes your mind for success, boosting your confidence and motivation to take action.

Remember Emily?

She recognised the importance of boosting her self-confidence to pursue her entrepreneurial dreams. By setting SMART goals and celebrating her achievements, she gained clarity and momentum in building her freelance business. Emily practiced self-compassion, embracing setbacks as learning opportunities rather than failures. Stepping out of her comfort zone, she networked with industry professionals and pitched her services to potential clients, gradually expanding her portfolio and clientele. Through visualization, Emily visualized herself thriving as a successful freelance graphic designer, fueling her confidence and determination to turn her dreams into reality.

My point?

As you navigate the journey of resigning from your current job and transforming your career, developing strategies to boost your self-confidence is paramount. By setting SMART goals, celebrating your achievements, practicing self-compassion, stepping out of your comfort zone, and visualizing success, you can cultivate unwavering confidence and unlock your full potential. Remember, confidence is not about being flawless but about trusting in yourself and your abilities to overcome obstacles and achieve your aspirations. With these strategies in your toolkit, you have the power to resign with confidence, transform your career, and reclaim your life.

Take a moment to reflect on your unique strengths, knowledge, skills, and experiences by creating a "Strengths Reflection" list.

Write down at least five qualities or achievements that highlight your capabilities and accomplishments.

Then, for each item on your list, jot down a brief explanation of how that strength has contributed to your success in the past or how it can support you in achieving your future goals. This exercise will not only reinforce your confidence in yourself but also remind you of the valuable assets you possess as you navigate your career journey.

Alternative Career Paths

If you're reading this book, then it's fair to say that you're thinking about exploring alternative career paths. Whether you're feeling stuck in your current job or simply curious about what else is out there, it's normal to have those feelings. Trust me, thousands of people have been in your shoes, wondering if there's something more fulfilling or exciting waiting for them in the world of work. And do you know what? Exploring alternative career paths can be a game-changer for you and your family. It's like opening a whole new world of possibilities where you get to choose the next chapter of your journey.

Why is it so important? Well, let me break it down for you.

First off, exploring alternative career paths gives you the chance to find something that truly lights you up inside. Think about it – we spend a big chunk of our lives working, so why not make sure it's something that makes us feel alive and excited to get out of bed in the morning? When you're stuck in a job that doesn't align with your passions or values, it can feel like you're just going through the motions, day in and day out. But by exploring different career paths, you can discover new opportunities that resonate with who you are and what you want out of life.

Secondly, exploring alternative career paths opens doors to new experiences and growth opportunities. Maybe you've always been curious about a certain industry or role but never had the chance to dive in and try it. Well, now's your chance! By stepping outside of your comfort zone and trying something new, you'll challenge yourself to learn and adapt in ways you never thought possible. Who knows – you might discover talents and passions you never even knew you had!

And finally, exploring alternative career paths empowers you to take control of your own career journey. Instead of feeling like you're at the mercy of whatever job happens to come your way, you get to be the captain of your own ship. You can set sail in whatever direction feels right for you, charting a course that's guided by your own dreams and aspirations. It's about taking ownership of your career and (your life) refusing to settle for anything less than what you deserve.

So, in this chapter, let's explore alternative career paths or it's all about finding fulfillment, embracing new opportunities, and taking control of your own destiny. It's a chance to break free from the status quo and create a career that's uniquely yours. And who knows where this journey might take you?

- It's your life.
- It's your career.
- You're in control.
- You make the decisions.
- You decide what's next for you…

The possibilities are endless – so why not take the first step and see where it leads?

Researching Different Industries, Roles, and Opportunities

Meet Maya. She's a creative powerhouse with a passion for design and a knack for storytelling. After years of working as a graphic designer in the advertising industry, Maya is ready for a change. She wants to explore new industries and roles that allow her to flex her creative muscles in exciting ways. But where should she start? Well, that's where researching different industries, roles, and opportunities comes into play.

First off, researching different industries gives Maya a chance to see what's out there beyond the advertising world. She's always been curious about the tech industry and how design intersects with cutting-edge innovation. Or she's intrigued by the world of sustainable fashion and wants to explore how her skills can make a positive impact on the environment. By diving into research, Maya can uncover new industries that align with her interests and values, opening doors to fresh possibilities she may never have considered before.

But it's not just about exploring industries – Maya also wants to discover new roles that allow her to leverage her design expertise in exciting ways. Sure, she's comfortable in her role as a graphic designer, but what if there's something even more fulfilling waiting for her? Maybe she'll stumble upon a role like "UX/UI Designer," where she can use her design skills to create seamless user experiences in digital products. Or she'll discover a role like "Brand Strategist," where she can combine her love for design with her passion for storytelling to help companies craft compelling brand narratives. The possibilities are endless, and researching different roles helps Maya uncover hidden gems that align perfectly with her skills and interests.

But it's not just about finding the right industry or role – Maya also wants to explore different opportunities within those spaces. Maybe, she's considering freelance gigs that allow her to work on diverse projects and be her own boss. Or she's interested in full-time positions at innovative startups that offer a demanding environment and opportunities for growth. By researching different opportunities, Maya can weigh the pros and cons of each option, finding the path that best suits her career goals and lifestyle preferences.

Strategies for Researching Different Industries, Roles, and Opportunities.

Now that we've talked about why researching different industries, roles, and opportunities is so important, let's dive into some practical strategies to help Maya (and you!) navigate this exploration process:

Online Resources. Maya can start by asking google and exploring online resources, and industry-specific websites to gather information about different industries, roles, and companies. These platforms offer job listings, company profiles, industry news, and insights from professionals working in various fields. Maya can use these resources to gain a better understanding of her options and identify potential opportunities that align with her interests and goals.

Networking. Maya can also tap into her network to gather insights and advice from professionals working in industries or roles that interest her. She can reach out to former colleagues, mentors, and industry contacts to request informational interviews or coffee chats. These conversations can provide valuable insights into different career paths, company cultures, and job opportunities, helping Maya make informed decisions about her next steps.

Professional Associations. Maya can explore joining professional associations and organizations related to her target industries or roles. These associations often offer networking events, workshops, and resources for members, providing opportunities to connect with professionals in their field of interest and stay updated on industry trends and opportunities. Maya can leverage these connections and resources to expand her network, gain insights into her desired career path, and access potential job opportunities.

Industry Events and Conferences. Maya can attend industry events, conferences, and workshops to immerse herself in her target industries and gain firsthand experience and insights. These events offer opportunities to learn from industry experts, network with professionals, and explore emerging trends and opportunities. Maya can use these experiences to broaden her perspective, make valuable connections, and discover new career opportunities that align with her interests and aspirations.

Mentorship. Maya can seek out mentorship from experienced professionals or mentors who can offer guidance, support, and advice as she explores different industries, roles, and opportunities. A mentor can provide valuable insights, share their experiences, and help Maya navigate challenges and decisions along her career journey. Maya can identify potential mentors through her network, professional associations, or mentorship programs offered by industry organizations or companies.

This is important…

Researching different industries, roles, and opportunities is a crucial step in the journey of exploring new career paths and finding the right fit for your skills, interests, and goals. By diving into research, you can uncover hidden opportunities, gain valuable insights, and make informed decisions about your next career move. Whether you're considering a career change, exploring new industries, or seeking growth opportunities, research is the key to unlocking new possibilities and here are a few more resources to consider:

Glassdoor - Glassdoor provides company reviews, salary information, interview insights, and job listings. It's an excellent resource for gaining insights into organizational culture, compensation packages, and potential career paths within various industries.

LinkedIn - LinkedIn is a professional networking platform that offers job listings, company profiles, industry news, and networking opportunities. It's an invaluable resource for connecting with professionals in your desired industries, conducting informational interviews, and exploring career paths.

Office of National Statistics - The ONS website offers comprehensive data on employment trends, industry growth projections, wage information, and occupational outlooks. It's a reliable source for understanding the current state of different industries and identifying emerging career opportunities.

Industry-specific Websites - Many industries have dedicated websites and publications that provide in-depth insights, news, and resources. For example, websites like TechCrunch for the tech industry, AdAge for marketing and advertising, or Health Leaders for healthcare offer industry-specific content, job listings, and trends analysis.

Professional Associations and Organisations - Professional associations, chartered institutes, trade associations and membership organisations related to your target industries often provide valuable resources, networking opportunities, and career development support. Membership in these organisations may grant access to industry events, job boards, educational resources, and mentorship programs. Examples include the institute of directors, Federation of small business, and your local chamber of commerce.

Yahoo Finance – This is a brilliant resource for researching industry trends and individual large corporate and publicly listed companies. With access to real-time market data, financial news, and analysis, users can stay informed about market trends and developments. Interactive charts and tools enable in-depth analysis of company performance and industry comparisons.

These online resources can serve as valuable tools for researching different industries, roles, and opportunities, helping you make informed decisions and navigate your career exploration journey effectively.

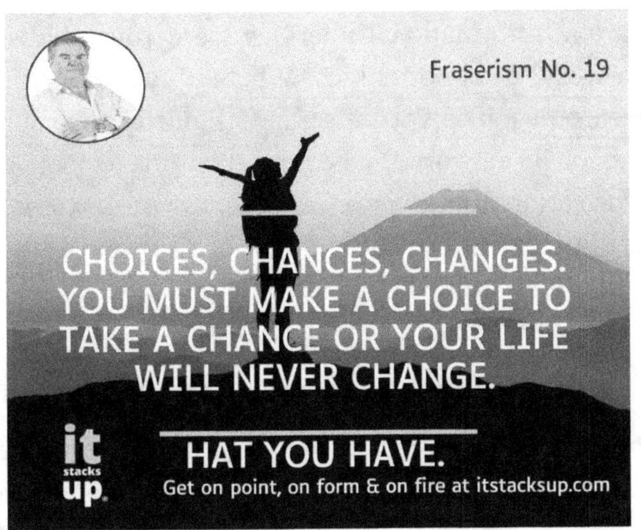

Challenge yourself to spend 15 minutes each day conducting research on industries, salaries, job descriptions, and job requirements related to your career interests.

Use online resources like Yahoo Finance, indeed.com, monster.com industry-specific websites, and facebook groups to gather information and insights. Keep a journal to document key findings, interesting trends, and potential opportunities you uncover during your research.

By committing to this daily research challenge, you'll deepen your understanding of your target industries, gain clarity on salary expectations, and identify roles that align with your skills and aspirations.

This exercise empowers you to take proactive steps towards advancing your career and making informed decisions about your professional path.

Networking and informational interviews are your golden tickets to unlocking a world of opportunities. Whether you're looking to resign from your current job, pivot into a new industry, or simply expand your professional network, mastering the art of networking and seeking informational interviews can propel you towards success in your career journey. So, let's dive in and discover how to leverage these powerful tools to make meaningful connections, gain valuable insights, and open doors to new possibilities.

Why Networking and Seeking Informational Interviews Matter

Meet Liam. He's a recent graduate with a passion for marketing and a desire to break into the tech industry. Unfortunately, Liam doesn't have a lot of experience under his belt, and he's feeling a bit overwhelmed about how to kickstart his career. Sound familiar?

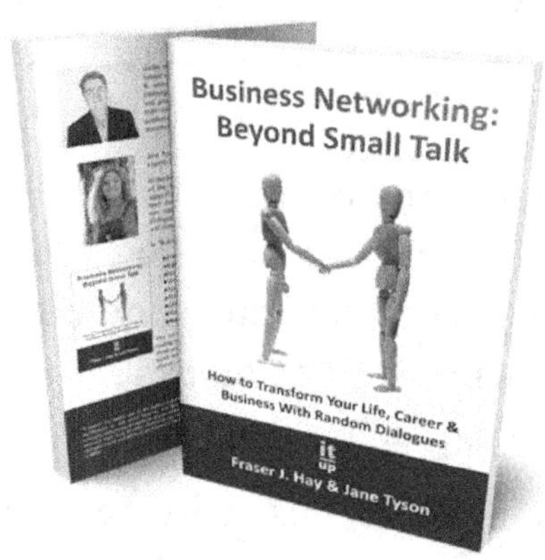

I do cover business networking in detail in my book *"**Business Networking: Beyond Small Talk**"* with Jane Tyson, but let's delve a little deeper into the context of you and your career.

First off, networking is all about building genuine relationships with people who can support and guide you on your career journey. Whether it's connecting with industry professionals on LinkedIn, attending networking events, or reaching out to alumni from your university, networking opens doors to new opportunities and insights you wouldn't have access to otherwise. For Liam, networking might involve reaching out to marketing professionals working in the tech industry to learn about their career paths, experiences, and advice for breaking into the field.

But networking isn't about asking for favours – it's also about giving back and offering support to others in your network. By being genuine, generous, and authentic in your interactions, you can cultivate meaningful connections that lead to valuable opportunities and collaborations down the road.

Now, let's talk about informational interviews. These are one-on-one conversations with professionals in your target industry or role, where you can learn more about their experiences, insights, and advice. Informational interviews are like treasure troves of wisdom and knowledge, giving you a behind-the-scenes look at what it's really like to work in a particular industry or role. For Liam, informational interviews might involve chatting with marketing managers, digital marketers, or product managers in the tech industry to gain insights into their day-to-day responsibilities, challenges, and opportunities for growth.

But here's the thing – informational interviews aren't job interviews. They're opportunities to gain experience, connect, and gather insights to inform your career decisions. So, approach them with curiosity, humility, and a genuine desire to learn from the experiences of others.

Now that we've talked about why networking and seeking informational interviews are important, let's dive into some practical strategies to help you master these skills and unlock new opportunities.

Leverage Your Existing Network. Start by tapping into your existing network of friends, family, classmates, professors, and colleagues. Let them know about your career interests and goals and ask if they can introduce you to anyone in their network who might be able to offer insights or guidance.

Use LinkedIn Strategically. LinkedIn is a goldmine for networking, so make sure your profile is polished and professional. Connect with professionals in your target industry or role, join industry-specific groups, and engage with relevant content to expand your network and stay top of mind.

Attend Networking Events. Keep an eye out for networking events, industry conferences, and professional meetups in your area. These events offer opportunities to connect with like-minded professionals, exchange ideas, and build relationships that can lead to new opportunities down the line.

Reach Out for Informational Interviews. Don't be afraid to reach out to professionals in your network or cold-email individuals whose careers you admire to request informational interviews. Be clear about your intentions, express genuine interest in learning from their experiences, and come prepared with thoughtful questions to make the most of your time together.

Follow Up and Stay Connected. The secret is in the follow-up. After networking events or informational interviews, be sure to follow up with a personalized thank-you message expressing gratitude for their time and insights. Stay connected with your network by sharing relevant articles, congratulating them on their accomplishments, and offering support whenever you can.

Networking and seeking informational interviews are powerful tools for advancing your career, making meaningful connections, and unlocking new opportunities. Whether you're looking to resign from your current job, pivot into a new industry, or simply expand your professional network, mastering the art of networking and informational interviews can open doors to new possibilities and accelerate your career growth.

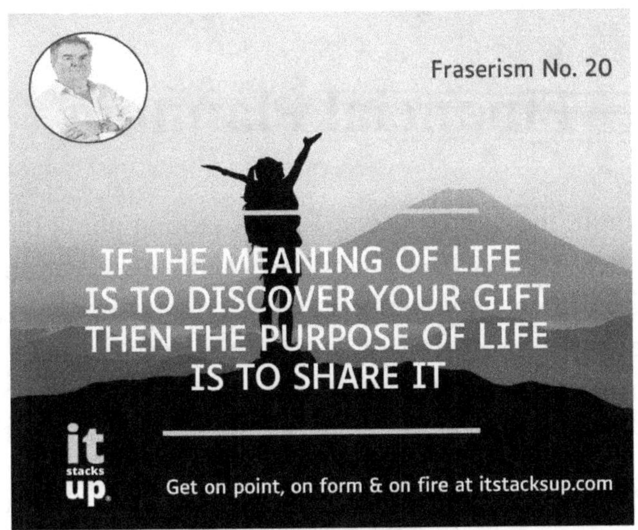

Create a networking action plan to proactively reach out to professionals in your desired industry or role and request informational interviews. Start by identifying at least five individuals or organisations you admire or would like to learn more about.

Craft personalised messages introducing yourself, expressing your interest in their work, and requesting a brief informational interview to gain insights and advice. Prepare a list of thoughtful questions to guide the conversation, focusing on topics such as career paths, industry trends, and advice for aspiring professionals.

Finally, outline your value proposition – what unique skills, experiences, and perspectives do you bring to the table? (And the problems you fix, and the potential impact of these going unaddressed.) By taking these proactive steps, you'll not only expand your professional network but also gain valuable insights and opportunities to advance your career journey.

Financial Planning

Let's talk about the money. Now, I know talking about money might not be the most thrilling thing in the world but stick with me because understanding financial planning is like having a superpower that can help you achieve your wildest dreams. So, let's break it down and explore why financial planning is so darn important.

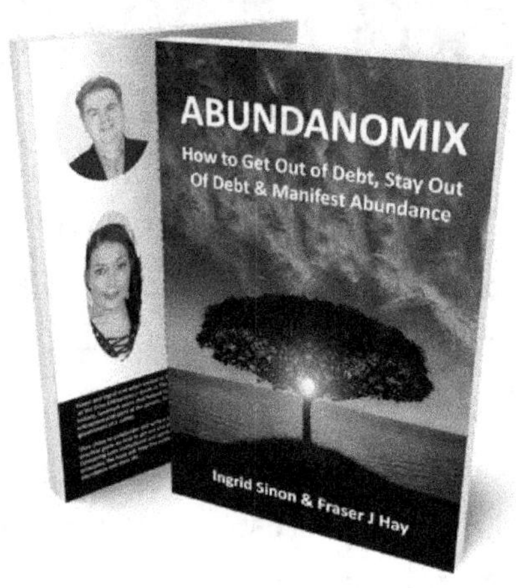

I do cover more about this in my book, "**Abundanomix,**" which I wrote with the CEO of a financial institutional after I did a speaking gig in the Seychelles, but for now, let's focus on some key points.

At its core, financial planning in the context of considering a career move (or in starting a business) is all about setting goals for your money and creating a roadmap to help you reach those goals. Whether it's saving for a dream vacation, buying a car, or even retiring early and living your best life, financial planning is the secret sauce that can turn your dreams into reality.

But why is it so important, you ask? Well, imagine this – you're cruising along in your career, feeling good about life, when suddenly, BAM! You're hit with an unexpected expense – your car breaks down, or you have a medical emergency. Without a solid financial plan in place, situations like these can throw a major wrench on your plans and leave you feeling stressed and overwhelmed.

But fear not, because that's where financial planning swoops in to save the day.

By creating a budget, setting aside money for emergencies, and planning, you can build a financial safety net that cushions you against life's curveballs. Plus, having a clear financial plan gives you peace of mind and empowers you to make smart decisions about your money, both now and in the future.

But financial planning isn't about preparing for the unexpected – it's also about seizing opportunities and making your money work for you. Whether it's investing in the stock market, saving for a down payment on a house, or starting your own business, a solid financial plan gives you the confidence and resources to pursue your passions and build the life you've always wanted.

Whether you're just starting out in your career or you're a seasoned pro, taking control of your finances and creating a plan is one of the best investments you can make in yourself. So, let's roll up our sleeves, crunch some numbers, and get ready to take on the world – because with a solid financial plan in place, the sky's the limit!

Creating a Budget and Assessing Your Financial Situation.

Trust me, this isn't about crunching numbers – it's about taking control of your money, building wealth, and paving the way for a bright future. So, grab your calculator and let's dive in!

Why is creating a budget so important? Picture this: you're cruising along in your career as a marketing strategist, scoring big wins left and right, when suddenly, you realise you've been spending more than you're making. Believe me, some people do live beyond their means, or simply don't have savings or planned for an unexpected crisis like getting laid off, paid, or fired. Without a budget in place, it's easy to lose track of where your hard-earned earnings are going — and you've worked hard for them. Right?

But fear not, because creating a budget enables you to take control of your financial destiny. Start by tracking your income and expenses — yes, every single one, from that morning Starbucks to your monthly rent (or mortgage). Once you've got a handle on where your money is coming from and where it's going, it's time to get down to business.

Use this tool to help you:

Download HERE

https://itstacksup.com/wp-content/uploads/2022/05/2022-NW-Statement.xlsx

In the context of resigning from your current job, creating a personal financial statement is essential for understanding your financial position and preparing for the transition.

It provides a comprehensive overview of your assets, liabilities, and net worth, enabling you to assess your financial stability and make informed decisions about your next steps. By having a clear understanding of your financial situation, including your savings, investments, and outstanding debts, you can determine how long you can sustain yourself financially without a steady income.

This information is invaluable when planning for potential expenses during a period of unemployment or while transitioning to a new job or career. Additionally, creating a personal financial statement allows you to identify areas where you may need to adjust your spending or saving habits to achieve your financial goals and maintain financial security throughout the transition process.

You will want to download this form to excel so you can update it regularly.

Making a note of all these items will help you to create your Personal financial statement.

Your personal financial statement should show assets and liabilities that you personally have.

have and not your business.

When you complete the form, ensure you sign & date it to let lenders and financial institutions know that you are sincere and accurate in your Statement and that it is up to date.

Step 1

Compile a list of all your assets regardless of whether they are fully paid up or not. Ensure

to enter the amount, you could receive if you were to sell that asset tomorrow.

Step 2

You need to compile a list of what you owe. If you have a list of creditors, this will help you.

Step 3

To calculate your net worth, simply subtract Your total liabilities from your total assets.

Net worth = Total Assets – Total liabilities

Assessing your financial situation is all about taking a good, hard look at your assets, liabilities, and overall financial health. Start by calculating your net worth – that's your total assets minus your total liabilities. This gives you a snapshot of where you stand financially and can help you track your progress over time.

Next, look at your debt – whether it's student loans, credit card debt, or a mortgage. Plan for paying off your debt as quickly as possible, starting with the highest interest rate loans first. And don't forget to build up an emergency fund to cover unexpected expenses – aim for at least three to six months' worth of living expenses saved up in a separate account.

Download HERE

https://itstacksup.com/wp-content/uploads/2022/05/2022-Monthly-Budget.xlsx

In addition to your personal financial statement, creating a personal monthly budget is crucial for managing your finances effectively during the transition period.

A monthly budget helps you track your income and expenses, allowing you to allocate your resources wisely and ensure that you can cover essential costs such as rent, utilities, groceries, and debt payments.

By outlining your expected income and planned expenses for each month, you can identify areas where you may need to cut back on spending or find ways to increase your income to make ends meet.

Additionally, having a clear budget in place enables you to prioritize saving for emergencies or unexpected expenses, providing you with financial stability and peace of mind as you navigate the uncertainties of resigning from your current job and seeking new opportunities.

How to Use this form:

1. Log Your monthly Income for you and your partner being as accurate as you can.

2. Make a note of how much you spend on bills, living costs and other expenses.

3. Think of different ways that you can reduce tour expenses using some of our tips.

4. If your income is weekly then perhaps do your calculations weekly & convert to monthly

5. Calculate your total income and enter it in the appropriate box below

6. Calculate your total monthly expenses and enter them in the appropriate box.

7. Your Net Amount available is calculated by Subtracting your expenses from income

Now, I know what you're thinking – creating a budget sound about as fun as watching paint dry. But trust me, it's not about restricting yourself or sucking the joy out of life – it's about making intentional choices that align with your goals and values. You're dreaming of buying your first home, traveling the world, or starting your own business. Whatever your dreams may be, a budget is your roadmap to getting there.

Start by identifying your fixed expenses – things like rent, utilities, and car payments – and then factor in your variable expenses, like groceries, dining out, and entertainment. Be honest with yourself about your spending habits and look for areas where you can cut back and save. It's swapping out fancy dinners for home-cooked meals or canceling that gym membership you never use. Every little bit counts!

But creating a budget isn't about cutting back – it's also about setting goals and priorities for your money. You want to save up for a down payment on a house, pay off your student loans, or invest in your future. Whatever your goals may be, break them down into manageable chunks and assign a dollar amount to each one. Then, set up automatic transfers or savings goals to make sure you're staying on track.

Finally, don't be afraid to ask for help if you need it. Whether it's meeting with a financial advisor, taking a personal finance course, or seeking out online resources and communities, there's a wealth of support available to help you on your financial journey. So, don't be shy – take the first step towards financial freedom today and start building the life of your dreams!

Here are five online resources that can also help you with financial planning when considering resigning from your job and pursuing a new one:

Personal Finance Blogs: Websites like The Balance, NerdWallet, or The Penny Hoarder offer comprehensive guides, articles, and tools for managing personal finances, including budgeting, saving, investing, and navigating career changes.

Financial Planning Calculators: Websites like Bankrate or SmartAsset provide a variety of financial planning calculators that can help you estimate expenses, savings goals, retirement needs, and more, allowing you to make informed decisions about your financial future.

Government Websites: Government websites such as the U.S. Department of Labor's CareerOneStop or the Small Business Administration offer resources and information on unemployment benefits, job training programs, small business loans, and other financial assistance options available during career transitions.

Job Search Platforms: Job search websites like Indeed or Glassdoor not only provide job listings but also offer salary information, company reviews, and career advice resources that can help you evaluate potential job opportunities and negotiate compensation packages.

Financial Planning Apps: Mobile apps such as Mint, YNAB (You Need a Budget), or Personal Capital offer budgeting tools, expense tracking features, and investment management solutions to help you stay organized and in control of your finances during a career change.

Utilising these online resources can provide you with valuable information, tools, and support to effectively manage your finances as you navigate the process of resigning from your current job and pursuing new career opportunities.

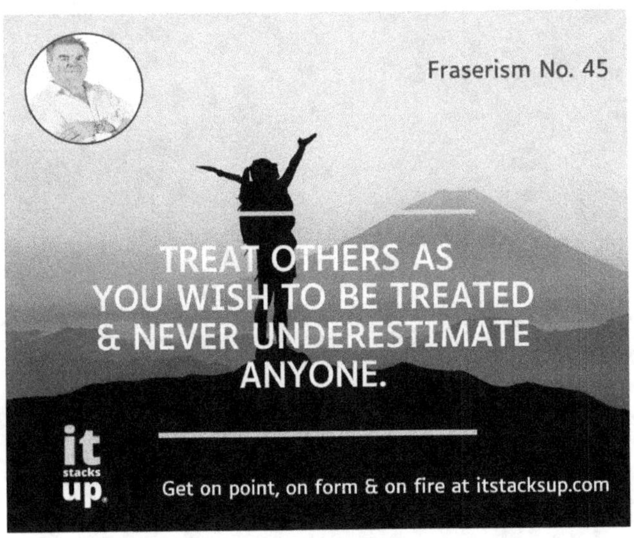

Take some time to download and complete the 2 tools shared at the start of this section. Get a copy of my book "Abundanomix" to help you get out and stay out of debt.

Explore the financial resources and support available to you during a career change. Start by researching online platforms, such as government websites, industry-specific forums, and financial blogs, to identify potential sources of financial assistance, including grants, scholarships, and low-interest loans.

Next, reach out to local community organisations, job centres, and professional associations to inquire about financial support programs tailored to individuals undergoing career transitions.

Finally, don't forget to explore opportunities for financial counseling or coaching services that can provide personalised guidance and support in managing your finances during this period of change.

Crafting Your Career Transition Plan

A transition plan can turn your dreams into reality and set you up for success as you navigate the twists and turns of your career path. So, grab your pen and paper, because we're about to dive into why crafting a transition plan is so darn important.

First things first, let's talk about what a transition plan is. At its core, a transition plan is like your roadmap to success – it's a step-by-step guide that helps you navigate the process of resigning from your current job and transitioning into a new role or career path. Whether you're leaving behind a toxic work environment, pursuing your passion, or simply craving a change of scenery, a transition plan provides the structure and clarity you need to make a smooth and successful transition.

But why is it so important, you ask? Well, picture this: you're standing at the edge of a cliff, ready to take the leap into the unknown. Without a transition plan in place, it's like jumping blindfolded – you have no idea where you'll land or how you'll get there. But with a solid plan in hand, you can approach your career transition with confidence, clarity, and purpose.

Crafting a transition plan isn't just about making a list of things to do – it's about setting goals, identifying obstacles, and developing strategies to overcome them. Start by clarifying your reasons for wanting to make a change and defining your career goals and aspirations. Then, assess your skills, strengths, and interests to determine your ideal career path and target industries or roles. Next, create a timeline for your transition, breaking down your goals into manageable steps and setting deadlines for each milestone. Finally, don't forget to consider the financial aspects of your transition, including budgeting for living expenses, saving for emergencies, and researching potential sources of income during your job search.

By crafting a transition plan, you'll not only gain clarity on your career goals and aspirations but also develop the confidence and resilience to navigate the challenges and uncertainties of your career transition. So, let's roll up our sleeves and get to work – because with a solid plan in place, the sky's the limit!

Setting SMART Goals for Your Career Transition: Mapping Your Path to Success

Before you dive headfirst into the unknown, let's talk about setting some SMART goals to guide your journey. Now, I know what you're thinking – what are SMART goals, and why do they matter? Well, buckle up, because I'm about to break it down for you.

First things first, let's talk about what SMART goals are. SMART is an acronym that stands for Specific, Measurable, Achievable, Relevant, and Time-bound. These are the five key criteria that make a goal SMART, and they're the secret sauce that can turn your dreams into reality.

So, let's break it down, shall we?

Specific. When setting your goals, be as specific as possible about what you want to achieve. Instead of saying "I want to find a new job," get specific about the type of job you're looking for, the industry you want to work in, and the skills you want to utilize or develop. For example, "I want to land a marketing manager position at a tech startup in the Strathclyde area of Scotland."

Measurable. Your goals should be quantifiable so that you can track your progress and measure your success. Think about how you'll know when you've achieved your goal and what metrics you'll use to evaluate your progress. For instance, if your goal is to increase your monthly income, you might set a specific target amount to aim for.

Achievable. While it's great to dream big, it's also important to set goals that are realistic and attainable. Consider your current skills, resources, and circumstances, and set goals that stretch you but are within your reach. For example, if you're looking to transition from a software engineer to a data scientist, you might set a goal to complete a data science certification program within the next six months.

Relevant. Your goals should be aligned with your values, interests, and long-term aspirations. Think about how each goal contributes to your overall vision for your career and life. For example, if your goal is to become a successful entrepreneur, you might set smaller goals related to building your business acumen, networking with industry leaders, and gaining relevant experience.

Time-bound: Finally, give yourself a deadline for achieving each goal to create a sense of urgency and accountability. Break down your goals into smaller, actionable steps with deadlines attached to each one. For example, if your goal is to land a new job within three months, set deadlines for updating your resume, networking with contacts, and submitting job applications.

By setting SMART goals for your career transition, you'll not only clarify your vision and focus your efforts but also increase your chances of success. So, grab your pen and paper, and make a note of some of these useful resources:

Trello: Trello is a versatile project management tool that allows users to create boards, lists, and cards to organize tasks and set SMART goals. Its visual interface makes it easy to track progress and collaborate with others during the career transition process.

Asana: Asana is another popular project management platform that can help individuals plan and set SMART goals for their career transition. With features such as task assignments, deadlines, and progress tracking, Asana enables users to stay organized and focused on achieving their objectives.

GoalsOnTrack: GoalsOnTrack is a comprehensive goal-setting app that guides users through the process of setting and achieving SMART goals. It provides tools for creating action plans, tracking progress, and staying motivated, making it an ideal resource for those navigating a career transition.

Strides: Strides is a goal and habit tracking app that allows users to set SMART goals, create action plans, and monitor progress over time. With customizable goal tracking features and insightful analytics, Strides helps individuals stay accountable and make meaningful progress towards their career goals.

Todoist: Todoist is a task management app that helps users organize their tasks, set deadlines, and prioritize activities to achieve their goals. With its intuitive interface and cross-platform compatibility, Todoist is an excellent tool for planning and executing SMART goals during a career transition journey.

Take a few minutes to grab a pen, paper, and jot down three career transition goals using the SMART criteria: Specific, Measurable, Achievable, Relevant, and Time-bound.

Start by identifying a specific industry or role you're interested in transitioning to, then determine measurable milestones such as obtaining relevant certifications or gaining experience in the field.

Ensure that each goal is achievable given your current skills and resources, relevant to your long-term career aspirations, and set a realistic time frame for completion. By setting SMART goals, you'll empower yourself to take actionable steps towards your career transition with clarity and purpose.

Creating a Timeline and Action Steps for Mapping Out Your Path to Success

Before you take the leap, let's talk about creating a timeline and action steps to ensure a smooth and successful transition. Now, I know what you're thinking – why do I need a timeline? Well, buckle up, because I'm about to break it down for you.

First off, creating a timeline is like plotting your course on a map – it helps you stay on track and navigate the twists and turns of your career transition with confidence and clarity. By setting specific deadlines for each step of the resignation process, you'll avoid procrastination and ensure that you're taking proactive steps towards your goals.

But why is it so important, you ask? Well, picture this: you're standing at the edge of a diving board, ready to take the plunge into the unknown. Without a timeline in place, it's like jumping blindfolded – you have no idea when you'll land or what awaits you on the other side. But with a clear timeline and action steps, you'll approach your resignation with confidence, knowing exactly what needs to be done and when.

So, grab your diary or phone calendar and let's start mapping out your path to success – because with a well-planned timeline and action steps, you will generate the confidence, progress and results you want in your life and career especially if you follow this process:

Step 1: Self-Assessment and Reflection

Reflect deeply on your career goals, values, and aspirations. Consider what truly motivates you and where you envision yourself in the future. For example, Samantha, a marketing coordinator in the healthcare industry, realized her passion for sustainability and decided to pursue a career in environmental advocacy.

Step 2: Research and Exploration

Explore diverse career paths, industries, and companies that align with your interests and goals. Dive into online resources, attend industry events, and connect with professionals in your desired field. For instance, John, a software engineer, researched opportunities in renewable energy and discovered a growing demand for tech professionals in the solar energy sector.

Step 3: Setting SMART Goals

Define specific, measurable, achievable, relevant, and time-bound goals for your career transition. Whether it's securing a new job, acquiring a certification, or building a professional network, set clear objectives to guide your journey. For example, Emily, a project manager, set a SMART goal to obtain her Project Management Professional (PMP) certification within six months to enhance her career prospects.

Step 4: Creating a Transition Plan

Develop a comprehensive transition plan outlining the steps needed to resign from your current job and transition smoothly to your new role or industry. Break down tasks into actionable steps, set deadlines, and prioritize your action items. For instance, Mark, a financial analyst, created a detailed plan to update his resume, network with industry professionals, and prepare for job interviews within a three-month time frame.

Step 5: Notifying Your Employer

Schedule a meeting with your supervisor or HR department to formally resign from your current job. Prepare a well-crafted resignation letter expressing gratitude for the opportunities and discussing your transition plan. For example, Jessica, a sales manager, notified her employer of her decision to resign and offered to assist with the transition process by training her replacement and documenting key processes.

Step 6: Transition Planning

Collaborate with your employer to create a seamless transition plan that ensures continuity of work and knowledge transfer. Delegate tasks, organize handover meetings, and provide necessary training to your colleagues or replacement. For instance, David, a customer service representative, collaborated closely with his team to delegate responsibilities and document customer inquiries to facilitate a smooth transition for his successor.

Step 7: Networking and Job Search

Kickstart your job search by networking with professionals in your target industry and exploring job opportunities online. Update your professional profiles, attend networking events, and leverage social media platforms to expand your connections. For example, Melissa, a graphic designer, attended industry conferences and joined online design communities to network with potential employers and showcase her portfolio.

Step 8: Finalising Your Transition

Wrap up any remaining tasks at your current job and prepare for your departure. Complete exit interviews, provide constructive feedback, and express gratitude to your colleagues and mentors. Leave on a positive note, maintaining professional relationships and leaving a lasting impression. For instance, Michael, a project coordinator, finalized his transition by completing handover documentation and expressing appreciation for his team's support throughout his tenure.

Step 9: Embracing Your New Role

Embrace your new role with enthusiasm and confidence. Take the time to acclimate to your new environment, build relationships with your colleagues, and seize opportunities for growth and development. Stay open-minded, adaptable, and proactive in navigating the challenges and opportunities that come your way. For example, Rachel, a marketing specialist, embraced her new role at a tech startup by immersing herself in the company culture, attending team-building events, and actively contributing innovative ideas to drive business growth.

By following this process and staying committed to your goals, you'll resign from your current job with confidence, transform your career, and reclaim control over your professional journey. Remember, each step is a building block towards your success, and with determination and perseverance, you'll achieve the confidence, progress and results you want in your life and career.

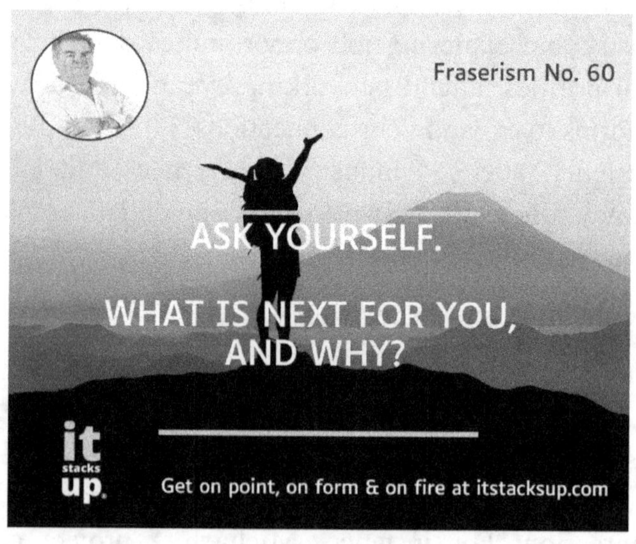

 Create your own timeline and action steps for resigning from your current job. Start by identifying your desired last day of work and work backward, outlining the tasks and milestones you need to achieve leading up to that date.

For example, set a deadline for drafting your resignation letter, scheduling a meeting with your supervisor, and completing any necessary handover tasks. Break down each action step into smaller, manageable tasks, and allocate specific times for completion.

By creating a personalized timeline and action plan, you'll gain clarity and confidence in navigating your resignation process with ease and efficiency.

Now, it's time for a summary of some of the other things we've covered so far to assist you with the planning for the logistical aspects of transitioning to a new career as they're just as crucial as the emotional and professional considerations.

It involves careful preparation and foresight to ensure a smooth and seamless transition from your current job, role, or position to the next phase of your career journey.

Let's dive into some key steps and considerations to help you navigate this process with confidence.

Step 1: Financial Planning

One of the first logistical aspects to address is your financial situation. Evaluate your current financial standing and consider how your transition will impact your income and expenses. Create a budget to track your finances during the transition period and identify any areas where you may need to cut back or save money. For example, Helen, an HR manager, decided to build up her savings before resigning from her job to give herself a financial buffer during her job search. So, ask yourself, how much savings do you have?

Step 2: Healthcare and Benefits

Consider how your transition will affect your healthcare coverage and other employee benefits. Review your current benefits package and determine when your coverage will end after resigning from your job. Explore alternative options for healthcare coverage, such as COBRA insurance or private health insurance plans. Additionally, consider any retirement accounts or pension plans associated with your current job and determine how they will be affected by your transition. For instance, Charles, a software developer, researched different healthcare plans available in his area and compared their costs and coverage options before deciding. Moneysavingexpert.com is an excellent resource to help compare different products and services you may wish to consider.

Step 3: Relocation Considerations

If your new career opportunity requires relocation, take the time to carefully plan and prepare for the move. Research potential relocation expenses such as moving costs, temporary housing, and transportation. Consider the impact of relocating on your personal life, family, and social connections, and weigh the pros and cons of the move. For example, Lisa, a project manager, researched rental prices and neighborhoods in her new city to find a suitable place to live that fit her budget and lifestyle preferences. Zoopla.com and Rightmove.com are two useful websites to help you with your property research.

Step 4: Professional Development and Training

As you transition to a new career, invest in your professional development and skill enhancement to increase your competitiveness in the job market. Identify any gaps in your skills or knowledge and seek out training programs, workshops, or certifications to address them. Consider joining professional organizations or networking groups related to your new career field to expand your connections and stay updated on industry trends. For instance, Mike, a graphic designer transitioning to web development, enrolled in an online coding bootcamp to learn new programming languages and enhance his technical skills.

Step 5: Legal and Contractual Obligations

Before resigning from your current job, carefully review any legal or contractual obligations that may affect your transition. Consider factors such as non-compete agreements, intellectual property rights, and confidentiality agreements, and consult with legal professionals if necessary. Ensure that you fulfill any notice periods or contractual requirements with your current employer to maintain a positive relationship and avoid potential legal issues. For example, Emily, a sales associate, reviewed her employment contract to understand her obligations regarding client confidentiality and non-solicitation clauses before resigning from her job.

For me, planning for the logistical aspects of transitioning to a new career requires thorough research, careful consideration, and proactive preparation. By addressing key factors such as financial planning, healthcare and benefits, relocation considerations, professional development, and legal obligations, you can navigate your career transition with confidence and set yourself up for success in your new role.

Remember to stay organised, flexible, and proactive throughout the process, and seek support from professionals and mentors as needed. With the right preparation and mindset, you can embark on a new career path and reclaim your life with confidence and enthusiasm.

Take a moment to create a checklist of logistical aspects to consider when transitioning to a new career. Consider factors such as financial planning, healthcare and benefits, potential relocation, professional development, and legal obligations.

For example, list items such as researching healthcare options, budgeting for relocation expenses, and identifying training programs to enhance your skills.

By proactively addressing these logistical considerations, you'll be better prepared to navigate your career transition with confidence and ease, ensuring a smooth and successful journey to your next professional chapter.

Managing the Resignation Process

Now, let's talk about managing the resignation process and why it's a crucial step in your career transformation journey.

Imagine that you're on a road trip to your dream destination, but before you can hit the open road, you need to carefully map out your route, plan your stops, and ensure you have everything you need for the journey ahead. Well, think of managing the resignation process as your roadmap to a successful career transition. It's all about navigating the twists and turns of resigning from your current job with grace and professionalism, while also setting yourself up for success in your next chapter.

So, why is managing the resignation process so important, you ask? Well, let me break it down for you. First and foremost, it's about leaving your current job on good terms and maintaining positive relationships with your employer and colleagues. Whether you've outgrown your role, found a new opportunity, or simply need a change, how you manage your resignation can have a lasting impact on your professional reputation and future career prospects.

But it's not just about the here and now – it's also about laying the groundwork for your future success. By managing the resignation process effectively, you can set yourself up for a smooth transition to your next job, minimize any potential disruptions or complications, and position yourself as a confident and capable professional ready to take on new challenges.

Let's not forget about the emotional aspect of it all. Resigning from your job can stir up a whirlwind of emotions – excitement, anxiety, uncertainty, you name it. But by managing the resignation process thoughtfully and intentionally, you can navigate these emotions with grace and confidence, knowing that you're making the best decision for your career and your future.

Let's delve into Pete's story to understand the emotional impact of resigning from a job.

Pete, a resolute project manager in offshore services, found himself in a challenging situation. Despite his passion for his work and commitment to his team, he faced constant micromanagement and criticism from his boss. Initially, Pete tried to brush off the negativity and focus on his tasks, but over time, the constant stress and pressure took a toll on his mental well-being.

He felt a mix of emotions – frustration, anxiety, and even self-doubt – as he grappled with the decision to resign. However, what finally made him choose to leave was a realization that staying in a toxic environment was hindering his growth and happiness.

Pete recognised that prioritising his mental health and professional fulfillment was the best decision for his career and future. With a heavy heart yet a sense of relief, Pete took the courageous step to resign, knowing that it was the first step towards a brighter and more fulfilling future.

My point?

Whether you're embarking on a new adventure or simply seeking greener pastures, remember that managing the resignation process is an essential step in your journey toward career fulfillment and personal growth. It's about taking control of your destiny, owning your decisions, and embracing the opportunities that lie ahead.

Deciding when and how to resign from your job.

Deciding when and how to resign from your job is a pivotal moment in your career journey, and it too needs a well-planned approach and strategy. Let me explore some key considerations to help you make this decision confidently.

Firstly, timing is key when it comes to resigning from your job. Take a step back and assess your current situation – are there any major projects or deadlines looming on the horizon? Consider the impact of your departure on your team and the company. Just like a software developer named Shirley working in the tech industry. She'd been offered an exciting opportunity at a startup, but her team is amid a critical product launch. In this scenario, now if were you, you might decide to wait until after the launch to resign, ensuring a smooth transition and minimizing any disruption to your colleagues.

Next, let's talk about the how of resigning – the method and approach you'll take to communicate your decision to your employer. While sending an email may seem convenient, opting for a face-to-face meeting or phone call is often more professional and respectful. This allows you to express your gratitude for the opportunities you've had and discuss your transition plan in person. Keep in mind that emotions may run high during this conversation, so it's important to stay composed and professional.

For instance, picture yourself as a production manager named James in the advertising industry. You've decided to resign due to a lack of growth opportunities, so you scheduled a meeting with your supervisor to discuss your decision. Despite feeling nervous, you approach the conversation with confidence and professionalism, leaving on good terms with your employer.

Additionally, consider the emotional aspect of resigning from your job. It's normal to feel a mix of emotions – excitement for the future, anxiety about the unknown, and even guilt about leaving your colleagues behind. Take the time to process these feelings and acknowledge that it's okay to feel uncertain about this big decision. Seek support from friends, family, or a mentor who can offer guidance and reassurance during this transitional period.

Let's say you're a project manager named Maya in the offshore oil and gas industry. You've been offered a new opportunity (with a competitor) that aligns better with your long-term goals, but you're feeling torn about leaving your team behind. In this situation, reaching out to a coach or mentor who has been through a similar experience can provide valuable perspective and support.

Deciding when and how to resign from your job requires careful consideration of timing, communication, and emotions. By approaching this process thoughtfully and strategically, you can navigate your resignation with confidence and professionalism, setting yourself up for success in your next career chapter. Remember, it's all about making the best decision for you, your family, and your career.

Reflect on your current job situation and consider when and how you would ideally like to resign. Start by assessing any upcoming projects, deadlines, or commitments at work and determine a suitable time for your resignation.

Next, think about how you would communicate your decision to your employer – whether through a face-to-face meeting, phone call, or email – and consider the potential emotional impact of your resignation.

Finally, jot down your thoughts and considerations, and use them to create a personalised plan for deciding when and how to resign from your job. By taking this proactive approach, you'll feel more empowered and confident in navigating this important career transition.

Communicating your resignation professionally and gracefully

This is often perceived as a difficult step in the process of leaving your job and transitioning to a new phase in your career. It's essential to manage this conversation with care and consideration to maintain positive relationships and leave a lasting impression. Let's explore some key strategies and tips for navigating this conversation with confidence and professionalism.

Choose the right time and place to communicate your resignation. Schedule a meeting with your supervisor or manager in a private setting where you can have a candid and uninterrupted conversation. Avoid announcing your resignation in a group setting or during a busy time when your manager may be preoccupied with other tasks. For example, imagine you're a graphic designer like Ryan in the creative industry. You've decided to resign due to a lack of growth opportunities, so you scheduled a one-on-one meeting with your manager, Fiona, to discuss your decision. By choosing the right time and place for the conversation, you can ensure that it's focused and respectful.

Approach the conversation with professionalism and clarity. Be direct and to the point about your decision to resign and avoid getting sidetracked by unrelated topics. Clearly communicate your reasons for leaving, whether it's for career advancement, personal growth, or a better fit elsewhere. Express gratitude for the opportunities you've had at the company and acknowledge any contributions you've made during your tenure.

Imagine if you were a software engineer like Carolyn in the technology sector. You've decided to resign because you've been offered a leadership position at another organisation. During your resignation conversation with your manager, you express appreciation for the support and mentorship you've received and explain that the new role aligns better with your long-term career goals.

It's also important to anticipate and address any questions or concerns your manager may have about your resignation. Be prepared to discuss your transition plan, including how you'll wrap up your current projects and train your replacement. Offer to assist with the transition process and provide any necessary documentation or information to ensure a smooth handover.

Imagine if you were like Paula - a sales manager in the retail industry. You've decided to resign because you're relocating to another city for family reasons. During your resignation conversation with your supervisor, you assure them that you'll complete any pending tasks and train your successor to ensure a seamless transition for the sales team.

Maintain professionalism and positivity throughout the resignation process, even if the conversation becomes emotional or challenging. Keep your emotions in check and avoid burning bridges or making negative remarks about the company or your colleagues.

Remember that the way you handle your resignation can impact your professional reputation and future career opportunities. Let's say you're a marketing coordinator named Alex in the hospitality industry. You've decided to resign because you've been offered a remote position that offers better work-life balance. Despite feeling sad to leave your team, you maintain a cheerful outlook during your resignation conversation and express gratitude for the experiences you've had at the company.

Personally, I think it's important that communicating your resignation professionally and gracefully is essential for leaving your job on good terms and transitioning to a new phase.

By choosing the right time and place for the conversation, approaching it with professionalism and clarity, addressing any questions or concerns, and maintaining positivity throughout the process, you can ensure a smooth and respectful transition for both you and your employer.

Here are five online resources that can assist in crafting resignation letters, and I include a template example for your perusal at the end.

The Muse. The Muse provides templates and guides for various professional documents, including resignation letters. Their resources offer tips on how to structure the letter effectively and provide examples to help you get started.

Indeed, Career Guide. Indeed's Career Guide section offers advice on all aspects of the job search process, including resigning from your current job. They provide templates and samples for resignation letters, along with tips on how to navigate the resignation process professionally.

Monster Career Advice. Monster's Career Advice section features articles and resources on writing resignation letters and managing the resignation process. They offer customizable resignation letter templates and guidance on how to tailor your letter to your specific situation.

LinkedIn Learning. LinkedIn Learning offers online courses on professional development topics, including writing effective resignation letters. These courses provide practical tips and strategies for crafting a compelling resignation letter that reflects your professionalism and gratitude.

Career Contessa. Career Contessa offers articles and resources on various career-related topics, including resigning from your job. They provide guidance on how to write a resignation letter that leaves a positive impression and maintains good relationships with your employer and colleagues.

These resources can be valuable tools in crafting a well-written and professional resignation letter that effectively communicates your decision to leave your current job.

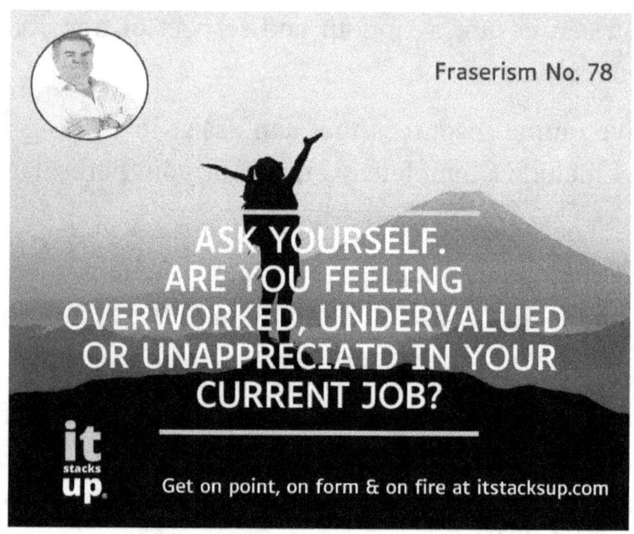

Sample Resignation Letter

Dear [Recipient's Name],

I am writing to formally resign from my position as [Your Job Title] at [Company Name], effective [Last Working Day, typically two weeks from the date of the letter]. After much consideration, I have made the difficult decision to pursue new opportunities that align more closely with my long-term career goals and personal aspirations.

I want to express my sincere gratitude for the opportunities I have had during my time at [Company Name]. I have learned and grown immensely both personally and professionally, and I am grateful for the support and guidance I have received from you and the entire team.

Please know that this decision was not made lightly, and I am committed to ensuring a smooth transition during my remaining time with the company. I am available to assist with training my replacement, completing any outstanding projects, and transitioning my responsibilities to ensure minimal disruption to the team.

I value the relationships I have built during my time at [Company Name] and hope to maintain those connections in the future. I look forward to staying in touch and continuing to support the company's success in any way I can.

Thank you once again for the opportunity to be a part of the [Company Name] team. I am grateful for the experiences I have had here and wish the company continued success in the future.

Sincerely,

[Your Name]

Feel free to edit the above template and tailor it to your current situation, job, and reasons for departure. Keep editing it until your head, heart and gut are aligned and that it feels right to you.

Navigating The Job Search Process

This is like embarking on a quest to find the perfect fit for your career. Picture this: You're standing at the edge of a forest, ready to explore the vast opportunities that lie ahead. Each path you take could lead to new adventures and possibilities.

Whether you're a high school graduate like Scott, who dreams of becoming a veterinarian, or a recent college graduate like Alex, who's eager to break into the tech industry, the job search process is an essential journey toward achieving your career goals. It's about more than just finding any job; it's about finding the right job – one that aligns with your skills, interests, and aspirations. For Scott, navigating the job search process means researching different veterinary clinics, networking with professionals in the field, and preparing a standout resume and cover letter.

As for Alex, it involves exploring job opportunities in the tech sector, building a strong online presence, and honing technical skills through relevant courses and certifications. No matter where you are in your career journey, mastering the art of navigating the job search process is crucial for unlocking new opportunities and taking your career to new heights.

It's all about seizing control of your future and making informed decisions that set you up for success. So, let's take a closer look…

Updating your resume, LinkedIn profile, and other materials

Think of this as polishing your professional image and putting your best foot forward as you prepare to take the next step in your career. Let's dive into why this is important and how you can approach it effectively.

Your CV (Resume) is like your personal marketing brochure – it's your chance to highlight your skills, experience, and accomplishments to potential employers. Take the time to review and revise your resume, making sure it accurately reflects your current job responsibilities, achievements, and skills. For example, imagine you're a marketing manager named Sophia in the fashion industry. You've decided to resign from your current job to pursue a career in digital marketing. As you update your resume, you highlight your experience with social media marketing campaigns, e-commerce strategies, and influencer partnerships to align with your new career goals.

Next, let's discuss updating your LinkedIn profile. In today's digital age, your LinkedIn profile is often the first impression you make on recruiters and hiring managers. Make sure your profile is up to date with your latest job title, responsibilities, and achievements. Add a professional profile photo and update your headline to reflect your career aspirations. Consider also optimising your profile with relevant keywords and skills to improve your visibility to recruiters. For instance, imagine you're a software engineer named Max in the technology sector. You've decided to resign from your current job to pursue a career in artificial intelligence. As you update your LinkedIn profile, you highlight your expertise in machine learning algorithms, neural networks, and programming languages like Python to attract opportunities in AI.

In addition to your resume and LinkedIn profile, don't forget to update other materials such as your cover letter, portfolio, and personal website. Your cover letter should be tailored to each job application, highlighting your qualifications and why you're a good fit for the role. Your portfolio should highlight your best work samples and projects relevant to your target industry or job position. And if you have a personal website or blog, make sure it reflects your professional brand and highlights your expertise in your field. Let's say you're a graphic designer named Emily in the design industry.

You've decided to resign from your current job to pursue freelance opportunities. As you update your materials, you create a portfolio website highlighting your design projects, client testimonials, and blog posts on industry trends and techniques.

For me, updating your resume, LinkedIn profile, and other materials is vital in preparing for your career transition. By taking the time to polish your professional image and highlight your skills and accomplishments, you'll position yourself as a strong candidate in the job market and increase your chances of success in landing your dream job.

Here are some resources to help you:

Zety Resume Builder. Zety offers a user-friendly resume builder with a wide range of customizable templates and formatting options. It also provides helpful tips and suggestions for crafting a compelling resume.

Resume.com. It offers a simple and intuitive resume builder with easy-to-use templates and design options. It also features a built-in content optimizer to help you tailor your resume for specific job opportunities.

Canva. Canva is a versatile design platform that offers a variety of customizable resume templates. It allows you to easily create visually appealing resumes with drag-and-drop functionality and access to a vast library of graphics and icons.

Novoresume. Novoresume provides a professional resume builder with customizable templates and sections for different types of resumes, such as chronological, functional, or combination. It also offers suggestions for optimizing your resume content.

Resume Genius. Resume Genius offers a comprehensive resume builder with step-by-step guidance and pre-written content for various industries and job titles. It also provides tools for customizing your resume and tailoring it to specific job descriptions.

Networking effectively and leveraging connections.

As mentioned in chapter 4, Networking effectively and leveraging connections is a powerful tool in your career transition toolkit. It's about building and nurturing relationships with professionals in your industry or target field to uncover new opportunities, gain insights, and expand your professional network. Let's re-visit why networking is essential and how you can do it effectively.

Imagine you're a recent college graduate named Tina who's passionate about environmental sustainability. You've decided to resign from your current job in retail to pursue a career in renewable energy. By attending industry events, joining professional associations, and connecting with professionals in the renewable energy sector, you can uncover job opportunities that may not be advertised publicly. For example, you might meet a sustainability manager named Tim at a renewable energy conference who informs you about an upcoming internship opportunity at his company. Networking helps you access these hidden job opportunities and gives you a competitive edge in the job market.

Or imagine if you are a social media marketing professional named Vera who's considering a career change to product management in the tech industry. By networking with product managers and tech professionals, you can gain valuable insights into the skills and experiences required for the role, industry trends, and potential challenges. For instance, you might connect with a product manager named Sharon who shares her career journey and offers advice on transitioning from marketing to product management. Networking allows you to learn from the experiences of others and make informed decisions about your career path.

Networking helps you establish a support system of mentors, peers, and advocates who can champion your career goals. Imagine you're a software engineer named Liam who's looking to transition from a traditional corporate environment to a startup. By networking with entrepreneurs, investors, and startup founders, you can find mentors who can provide guidance and support as you navigate the startup ecosystem. For example, you might meet a serial entrepreneur named Angus who offers to mentor you and introduce you to potential co-founders and investors. Networking allows you to build meaningful relationships with individuals who can support you in achieving your career aspirations.

Networking fosters opportunities for collaboration and professional development. Let's say you're a project manager named Noah who's passionate about social impact. By networking with professionals in the nonprofit sector, you can explore opportunities to collaborate on projects and initiatives that align with your values and interests. For instance, you might connect with a nonprofit director named Olivia who invites you to join a task force focused on environmental conservation. Networking opens doors to new collaborations and learning experiences that can enrich your career journey.

Again, in my book "Business Networking: Beyond Small Talk," Jane and I share practical tactics for leveraging your business networking for maximum confidence, impact, and results.

For me, networking effectively and leveraging connections is a critical component of resigning with confidence and transforming your career. By building and nurturing relationships with professionals in your industry or target field, you can uncover hidden job opportunities, gain insights and advice, establish a support system, and foster collaborations for professional development. So, don't underestimate the power of networking – invest in building meaningful connections and watch your career soar!

After reading about the importance of business networking, take a moment to identify three professionals in your desired industry or field whom you admire or would like to connect with. Also feel free to connect with me on Linkedin at https://www.linkedin.com/in/fraserjhay/

Then, reach out via LinkedIn or email with a personalised message expressing your interest in their work and requesting a virtual coffee chat or informational interview.

Use this opportunity to learn more about their career paths, seek advice, and explore potential collaboration opportunities. Remember, networking is about building genuine relationships and offering value, so approach each interaction with curiosity, authenticity, and a willingness to learn.

My book called "Pipeline" about Linkedin may also be of interest. It's here:

https://www.amazon.co.uk/Pipeline-prospecting-generates-expensive-advertising-ebook/dp/B06XTXH2XF/

Interviewing tips and techniques for securing a new job.

Now, regarded by many as one of the hardest parts of the job search process: interviews. Think of interviews as your time to shine, to show off all your amazing qualities and skills.

Whether you're a high school graduate like Anne, looking for your first part-time job at the local coffee shop, or a college student like Alex, aiming for a summer internship in finance, mastering the art of interviewing is super important for landing that dream job. It's not just about answering questions – it's about making an impression and convincing the interviewer that you're the perfect fit for the role. But don't worry, with the right tips and techniques, you'll be ready to knock those interviews out of the park and secure the job of which you've been dreaming.

So, let's dive into some interviewing tips and techniques that will help you stand out from the crowd and land your next big opportunity and at the end of this chapter, I'll give you a link to a video that you might just like. But first…

A comprehensive guide on interviewing tips and techniques for securing a new job:

Interviewing for a new job can be a daunting task, but with the right preparation and strategies, you can increase your chances of success. In this guide, we'll explore the top 15 most popular interview questions, the reasons for asking them, and the best answers to give to each, with examples to illustrate their effectiveness.

1. Tell me about yourself.

Reason for asking: This question allows the interviewer to learn more about you beyond your resume and assess your communication skills.

Good answer: "Sure! I'm an experienced project manager with over five years of experience in the software development industry. In my previous role at Tech Solutions, I led a team of developers to successfully launch several high-profile projects, resulting in a 20% increase in client satisfaction."

2. Why do you want to work here?

Reason for asking: Employers want to gauge your interest in their company and assess your alignment with their values and culture.

Good answer: "I'm excited about the opportunity to join XYZ Company because of its innovative approach to solving industry challenges. I admire your commitment to pushing the boundaries of technology and believe my skills in project management align perfectly with your goals."

3. What are your strengths?

Reason for asking: This question helps the interviewer understand what you bring to the table and how you perceive your own abilities.

Good answer: "One of my greatest strengths is my ability to effectively communicate and collaborate with cross-functional teams. I'm also highly organized and excel at prioritizing tasks to meet deadlines."

4. What are your weaknesses?

Reason for asking: Employers want to assess your self-awareness, honesty, and ability to acknowledge areas for improvement.

Good answer: "While I'm generally confident in my abilities, I've found that I can sometimes be overly critical of my own work. However, I've been actively adopting a more positive mindset and seeking feedback from others to help me improve."

5. Can you tell me about a time when you faced a challenge & how you overcame it?

Reason for asking: This question evaluates your critical thinking skills, resilience, and ability to handle adversity.

Good answer: "At my previous job, we encountered a major setback when our primary vendor failed to deliver a crucial component on time. I immediately convened a meeting with stakeholders to brainstorm alternative solutions, and we ultimately sourced the component from a different supplier, allowing us to meet our deadline and avoid project delays."

6. Where do you see yourself in five years?

Reason for asking: Employers want to understand your long-term career goals and aspirations to ensure alignment with the company's objectives.

Good answer: "In five years, I see myself taking on a leadership role within the company, leveraging my experience and expertise to drive strategic initiatives and mentor junior team members. I'm committed to continuous learning and growth and believe XYZ Company offers ample opportunities for advancement."

7. Why should we hire you?

Reason for asking: This question challenges you to articulate your unique qualifications and what sets you apart from other candidates.

Good answer: "You should hire me because I bring a combination of technical expertise, leadership skills, and a proven history of delivering results. I'm passionate about contributing to the success of your team and am confident that my background in project management makes me an ideal fit for this role."

8. How do you handle stress or pressure?

Reason for asking: Employers want to assess your ability to remain calm, focused, and effective in challenging situations.

Good answer: I thrive in fast-paced environments and see pressure as an opportunity to demonstrate my resilience and problem-solving abilities. I prioritize tasks, break projects down into manageable steps, and seek support from colleagues when needed to ensure successful outcomes."

9. Do you work better independently or as part of a team?

Reason for asking: This question helps the interviewer understand your preferred work style and how you collaborate with others.

Good answer: "I value both independent work and collaboration with a team. I'm self-motivated and enjoy taking ownership of projects, but I also recognize the importance of teamwork in achieving shared goals. I believe in leveraging the strengths of each team member to drive collective success."

10. Can you provide an example of a time when you demonstrated leadership skills?

Reason for asking: Employers want to evaluate your ability to lead, inspire, and influence.

Good answer: "Absolutely! In my previous role, I was tasked with leading a cross-functional team to implement a new software system.

I took charge of the project, delegating tasks effectively, and fostering open communication among team members. As a result, we successfully launched the system ahead of schedule and received praise from senior management for our collaboration and efficiency."

11. What motivates you?

Reason for asking: This question provides insight into what drives you and how you're likely to perform in the role.

Good answer: "I'm motivated by challenges that push me out of my comfort zone and opportunities to make a meaningful impact. I thrive in environments where I can continuously learn and grow, and I'm excited about the prospect of contributing to the success of your team."

12. How do you handle constructive criticism?

Reason for asking: Employers want to assess your ability to accept feedback, learn from it, and adapt your behavior.

Best answer: "I view constructive criticism as an opportunity for growth and welcome feedback from colleagues and supervisors. I actively seek out input on my performance and use it to identify areas for improvement. By remaining open-minded and receptive to feedback, I strive to continuously develop my skills and capabilities."

13. Tell me about a time when you had to multitask or prioritize tasks.

Reason for asking: This question evaluates your organizational skills, time management, and ability to handle multiple responsibilities.

Good answer: "In my previous role, I often had to juggle multiple projects simultaneously while also meeting tight deadlines. To prioritize tasks effectively, I would assess the urgency and importance of each task, create a timeline for completion, and allocate resources accordingly. By staying organized and adaptable, I was able to successfully manage competing priorities and deliver quality results."

14. Can you describe a situation where you had to resolve a conflict with a client?

Reason for asking: Employers want to assess your people skills, conflict resolution abilities, and professionalism (with clients and potentially colleagues too.)

Good answer: "Certainly! There was a disagreement with a colleague over the direction of a project, which was causing tension within the team. I initiated a one-on-one meeting with the colleague to discuss our perspectives openly and listen to their concerns. Through active listening and empathy, we were able to find common ground, compromise on a solution, and move forward collaboratively, ultimately strengthening our working relationship."

15. What do you know about our company?

Reason for asking: This question evaluates your research and preparation for the interview and assesses your interest in the company.

Good answer: "I've done extensive research on XYZ Company and am impressed by your commitment to innovation and customer satisfaction. I admire your recent initiatives to expand into new markets and your focus on sustainability. I'm excited about the opportunity to contribute to your team and be part of your continued success."

For me, preparing thoughtful responses to these common interview questions and highlighting your skills, experiences, and enthusiasm for the role and company, you'll be well-equipped to navigate the interview process with confidence and secure the job you desire. Remember to practice your responses, remain composed and professional, and let your authentic self shine through during the interview.

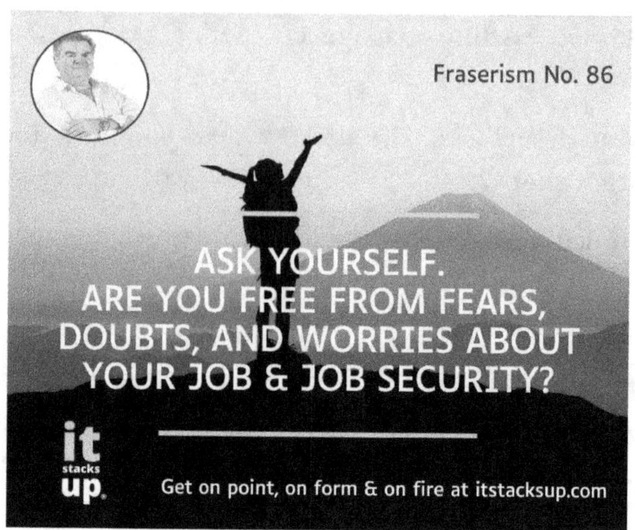

After learning about interviewing tips and techniques, take some time to conduct mock interviews with a friend or family member. Practice answering common interview questions and receiving feedback on your responses.

Pay attention to your body language, tone of voice, and overall presentation. Use this opportunity to refine your answers and build confidence in your interview skills. By simulating real interview scenarios, you'll be better prepared to ace your next job interview and secure the position you desire.

Wee Bonus. Watch this video. Listen. Relate. Assimilate as you make notes & apply.

To watch the video, visit
https://youtu.be/GonWas0boV8?si=NlrcxAjF8QS9TivI

Thank You

As we wrap up our journey of considering resigning with confidence, I want to take a moment to thank you for joining me on this journey. I also ask you to reflect on the insights I have shared and the transformative potential that lies ahead.

Depending on the option(s) you pursue, this could become the most exciting chapter of your career, and I mean that sincerely. I would like nothing better than to help you get on point, on form, and on fire to transform your career, leave your job and reclaim your life even if that means helping you at the start and each stage of your entrepreneurial journey.

Re-Read. Relate. Assimilate & apply.

It can pay great dividends to re-read the book and complete each of the exercises and activities. Tor armed with knowledge and determination, you have the power to overcome these obstacles and unlock your full potential. Addressing each cause offers us a pathway to growth and self-discovery.

In writing this book, my greatest hope is that you've found resonance in these words, that you've recognised aspects of yourself (or your work colleagues) and your experiences in your current job. For in that recognition lies the seed of transformation.

I urge you to take these insights to heart, to assimilate them into your daily life, and to apply them with unwavering commitment. Whether you're striving for personal excellence, want to leave an organisation for a new opportunity, (or even start a business), the principles outlined here hold the key to your personal, professional, and commercial success.

I share a lot more help, guidance, and support for each stage of the entrepreneurial journey in my other books, and I want to remind you just as I say in my TEDx talk- You're not just a human being, but a human becoming. What do you want to become next on your journey?

But to reach it, we must be willing to take the first step, to embrace the journey with courage and conviction. So, dear reader, remember this: the power to change lies within each of us.

Afterall, you already have the power, you just need reminding occasionally how to use it and breakthrough the barriers of personal, professional, and professional success.

Let's make your next career choice, the best you've ever made.

Oh, and if you, or any member of your team or staff need help, then get in touch.

Fraser J. Hay

www.itstacksup.com

One Last Thing...

Have you found **value** and **benefit** from reading this book and in being introduced to different ways to unify and simplify the management of your marketing?

Do you think others struggling with marketing ideas would find a **benefit** from reading this book if they didn't know about the software solutions I share?

Would you be prepared to **recommend** my book to others, or be prepared to write a positive review about it?

Who would be the first two people that you know that might be struggling with one or a combination of the causes and barriers we've discussed, who might benefit from reading this book?

Feel free to direct them to my book. I really do hope you have gotten value from my book. You will if you choose to act and start making changes to your marketing approach with the ideas I've shared.

Take a moment, reflect on this book, and write down the top 5 key "takeaways" you've gained from this book. Write what you've learned and consider adding a review of the book, for amazing things are about to start happening when you begin embracing and applying the principles contained herein, and my other books.

Even better, add a video review or testimonial and ping me the URL and in return I'll give you a wee personal thank you.

In addition to adding a review, consider sharing your thoughts via your online networks such as LinkedIn, Facebook, and X (twitter). If you believe what you've read is worth sharing, then please would you take a few seconds to let your colleagues know about it? If it can have a positive impact on their life or work, they'll be incredibly grateful to you.

And remember, if you've got questions, or are planning a corporate event or training day and require a keynote speaker then please do get in touch.

Fraser J Hay

www.itstacksup.com

About The Author

Fraser Hay is a seasoned business coach, consultant, and keynote speaker, recognised for his multi-award-winning entrepreneurship and global impact. Having been employed in both the public and private sectors, started and exited businesses (including an IPO).

He has delivered inspiring keynotes on four continents and authored over 20 books available on Amazon, Fraser is dedicated to empowering individuals, managers, and founders to conquer personal, professional, and commercial challenges at every stage of their entrepreneurial journey.

With an innovative approach to coaching, consultancy, and technology solutions, Fraser helps individuals and entrepreneurs realise their vision without struggle, limitation, or fear. Drawing from his extensive 30+ years' experience, Fraser has identified and tackled over 2000 common issues, challenges, and obstacles encountered in the workplace and on each stage of the entrepreneurial journey including starting a business with £10 and exiting.

Unlike traditional coaches, Fraser's methodology is grounded in practical solutions, documented insights, and guaranteed progress. Through webinars, keynote speeches, workshops, and coaching programs, he shares his wealth of knowledge and expertise to facilitate transformative growth for his clients.

As a TEDx keynote speaker with two decades of remote working experience, Fraser is committed to supporting owners, founders, and senior management teams in achieving their marketing objectives. He provides clarity, purpose, and measurable results, ensuring progress at every stage of the journey.